RUTH RUDNER is a frequent contributor to the *Wall Street Journal's* "Leisure & Arts" section, with pieces focussing mainly on Montana and the American West. Her other books include **Partings** and **Greetings from Wisdom, Montana.** She lives in Bozeman, Montana.

A
CHORUS
OF
BUFFALO

A CHORUS OF BUFFALO

Ruth Rudner

Bb

BURFORD BOOKS

Printed in the United States of America

10 9 8 7 6 5 4 3 2 1

Library of Congress Cataloging-in-Publication Data
Rudner, Ruth.
    A chorus of buffalo / Ruth Rudner.
        p.   cm.
    ISBN 1-58080-049-1 (hc.)
    1. American bison.   2. American bison—Yellowstone
National Park.   I. Title.
QL737.U53 R84   2000
599.64'3—dc21   99-088014

This is for BRUCE DETRICK

Orpheus
"He looked around
and the earth looked good
but it needed something
and it always would . . ."

CONTENTS

PREFACE—THE POLITICS OF BUFFALO

I WANTED the stories in this book to paint a portrait of the buffalo. I wanted a reader to know this animal; to ride with me through the Yellowstone backcountry, watching buffalo on vast, primeval meadows; seeing this gorgeous animal at home in an amazing landscape; at home there for 10,000 years. Just that. I did not want to write about the complicated politics surrounding buffalo.

But the political struggle over buffalo is a fact of life. There was no way to write many of these stories without mentioning aspects of it. I tried to do it in passing until my editor suggested that some stories were not clear without more fully explaining the controversy behind them.

I will try to do that here, perhaps simplifying it beyond what seems respectful of the many people who have now devoted years of their lives to these issues. I mean no disrespect. In my own way, I have also been watching buffalo for years. I've attended hearings dealing with the Yellowstone problems and interviewed people on all sides of that controversy for articles.

The buffalo controversy is, nominally, about brucellosis, a bovine bacterial disease transmitted during reproductive events. Buffalo became carriers of the brucellosis organism through contact with domestic cattle in the early days of Yellowstone Park, when cows were kept to provide milk for visitors and workers there. Many buffalo carry antibodies indicating exposure to brucellosis, although they do not themselves have the disease. A small fraction of buffalo are actually capable of transmitting the *brucella* organism.

In domestic cattle, brucellosis can cause a cow to abort her first calf. It also causes undulant fever in humans, an incurable and periodically debilitating disease. The most common victims are veterinarians who have worked with infected cattle, or, in more recent years, consumers of unpasteurized goat's milk and cheese from chronically infected Mexican goats.

Cattle states have spent huge amounts of money and time ridding domestic herds of the disease. States classified as "brucellosis-free" do not want that status endangered. For the individual rancher, brucellosis can be a catastrophe, because if even one cow in a herd tests positive for the disease, the rancher's entire herd must be destroyed.

The livestock interests would not be concerned if Yellowstone's buffalo stayed inside the park. But buffalo roam. Especially in a hard winter, they are apt to cross park boundaries to lower valleys in search of grass. Because the park is largely surrounded by public land (national forest), this should not be a problem, but there are grazing leases on some of that land, as well as private land abutting it. Areas attractive to buffalo are some of the same areas grazed by domestic cows in other seasons. Except in the Tetons, where cattle grazing land was grandfathered into the national park, buffalo and cattle are not in those areas at the same time.

Numerous environmental organizations and private individuals would like to see the public lands surrounding the park made available to bison. These public lands do not have cows on them in winter and most of the spring. Furthermore, the U.S. Forest Service has stated it will not allow cattle on those lands until 30 to 60 days after the buffalo have gone.

Buffalo and cattle have a relationship extending back about twenty-two million years. They are capable of mating. An erstwhile Montana state veterinarian talked to me several years ago about the theoretical possibility of a bull buffalo passing the disease to a domestic cow in the mating process. It is also possible for cows, grazing among the afterbirth materials of an infected buffalo, to ingest the bacteria, although this is highly unlikely given the fact that the *brucella* organism has limited viability outside its host and is quickly killed by direct sunlight. That same vet, however, suggested the organism could remain frozen for months in a patch of old snow lying in the shade, then come to life in a sudden moment of summer sun.

There is, however, *no known instance of transmission from wild buffalo to domestic cattle.* No one can produce a credible scientific study that proves transmission of brucellosis from buffalo to domestic livestock under natural pasture conditions, not even in the Tetons, where the animals mingle.

The federal Animal and Plant Health Inspection Service (APHIS)—the agency charged with setting national standards for domestic animal health—maintains the risk of brucellosis transmission is so slight that there is no harm in buffalo and cattle using the same areas so long as it is not at the same time. In spite of this, and the lack of evidence I've already mentioned, the Montana Stockgrowers Association and the Montana Department of Livestock (DOL) insist the risk is real. Frightened of sanctions imposed on Montana cattle by other states—an event over which the Montana state vet actually has some control—they have gone to battle with a vengeance, declaring that all Montana ranchers are at risk if the state loses its brucellosis-free status.

APHIS does not have the authority to remove a state's brucellosis-free status merely because brucellosis exists in wildlife. At the end of March 1999, a new APHIS regulation specifically stated that even if an infection occurs in one herd, APHIS will not take away a state's brucellosis-free status unless it appears in a second herd.

It is this controversy over brucellosis that makes it into the press; that gets talked about at meetings. In fact, there is a broader political agenda here; one that has to do with big government and states' rights; with what westerners consider the "taking" of their land, public or not. (The Fifth Amendment says that *private* property cannot be taken for public use without just compensation.)

The regional administrator of the eighth district EPA, Bill Yellowtail, is a Crow Indian who ranches on the Crow Reservation. He knows firsthand the concerns of ranchers. A former Montana state senator, he is well versed in Montana's politics. What the DOL and the ranchers are really saying, he offers, is that "we don't want government suggesting to us how we ought to be managing the natural resource, including the *public* natural resource."

In this scenario, the buffalo is another spotted owl, a gray wolf, a blacktail prairie dog—an animal interfering with a perceived God-given right to override the earth's needs if it interferes with how we do business. In a healthy ecosystem, all the components—animals, plants, people, soil, air, fire, water—are extant. In a failing ecosystem—one in which humans set themselves up as knowing more than the earth, more than God, more than the whole history of life on this planet—animals, plants, rivers, and mountains become expendable. They are seen as subservient, there to do the bidding of humans.

Each of these animals—owl, wolf, prairie dog, buffalo—provides a talisman to brandish for the westerner concerned with "states' rights." As we have become sophisticated in utilizing fear in our political tactics, these animals have become powerful symbols, arousing huge passions.

Fear and *fact* are both four-letter words, but they have little to do with one another. The rhetoric employed by the Department of Livestock and many ranchers and legislators is often devoid of scientific fact or logic or responsibility to the larger community, both ecological and

5

sociological. Fear directs the rhetoric. And anger. A rancher who may not agree with his neighbors has almost no
choice but to go along with them. He depends upon them
in an emergency. Good neighbors are one of the blessings
of life in the West. They are also a necessity.

Those people fighting for the buffalo's right to life and
livelihood are frequently dismissed as easterners, people
who don't know nothin' about raisin' cows. And effete
besides. In actual fact, most of the buffalo partisans live as
thoroughly and as connectedly in the region as do the
ranchers. There are, however, plenty of people across the
U.S. who have joined in the fight to protect the buffalo's
right to life. The animal is, after all, an *American* symbol. To
the extent that wild animals (or wild land) can ever "belong"
to anyone, they belong to *all* the people of this country.
People *know* that. When the draft Environmental Impact
Statement (EIS) that will ultimately determine buffalo
management for the next 15 years (once it is adopted) finally appeared in June 1998, it garnered 67,520 comments. Of
those, 63,000 came from all the U.S. states; the rest from a
number of foreign countries. The large majority of comments wanted protection for the buffalo.

Some ranchers say they don't mind buffalo. Some of
the livestock officials say the same thing. They even *like*
them, they say, so long as they stay inside park boundaries,
forgetting that buffalo are migratory animals. But they are
filled with a kind of party-line venom when, testifying at
hearings on the issue, they let fly with their comments on
how Yellowstone's buffalo are managed, or, in their view,

mismanaged, or on how they feel about public land outside of the park being used by buffalo. Interestingly, they usually introduce themselves as third- or fourth-generation Montanans, as if that gave them more claim to the land, and to knowledge about how it works, than those of us who may only have been here for five or twenty or fifty years. A flaw in this approach (for them) they seem not to have noticed is its recognition of the Indian as the de facto authority on how the land should be used. Anyone claiming that time on the land gives them certain rights needs to acknowledge that Indians have been here a good deal longer than three or four generations. As Donald Meyers, a Chippewa-Cree who is the game warden supervisor on the Rocky Boy's Reservation, noted in testimony at an EIS hearing, "I'm a millionth-generation Montanan."

For all the extreme polarization of the buffalo issue, the tension between private property and the public interest is not necessarily unhealthy. In forcing people to really *look* at what is happening, it offers a check on the megalomania of a one-sided view. *Any* one side. Sometimes the public interest, in its zeal, may indeed step too far into private property that is, in fact, managed with good stewardship. Many ranchers, meticulous caretakers of their land, are sensitive to the needs of wildlife. Many others are struggling to come to grips with a world radically changed from the one their fathers and grandfathers worked. Regardless of whom you listen to, and regardless of which side you think you are on, the trick is to discern what is truth and what is purely rhetoric, or, worse, distortion.

In an odd way, the draft EIS pulled people together—in knowing what they didn't want. *Everybody*—ranchers, environmentalists, Indians, legislators—objected to the preferred alternative proposed by the federal and state agencies. The environmental organizations, and many individuals, were distressed that it would continue the killing of buffalo that leave the park, as well as give continued control of buffalo to the DOL. The livestock interests thought it did not go far enough in protecting them from brucellosis, or in controlling the migration of buffalo from the park.

The Greater Yellowstone Coalition, an environmental organization working on this issue for over nine years in cooperation with 16 other organizations, including the InterTribal Bison Cooperative, the National Wildlife Federation, the Wilderness Society, and Defenders of Wildlife, came up with a citizens' plan that is a common-sense approach designed to benefit everyone—buffalo *and* people. There were several other similar plans presented as well, one of them by the Gros Ventre and Assiniboine of the Fort Belknap Reservation, where there is a herd of about 400 buffalo. The DOL and many of the ranchers want some combination of other, even less buffalo-friendly, alternatives in the EIS.

As of this writing, the DOL continues trapping buffalo (on forest service land) exiting the park's west side, in spite of the forest service waiting time between buffalo and cattle. The trapped animals are tested for brucellosis; those testing positive are shipped to slaughter. The test, however, is not very accurate. When more extensive testing of 19 animals killed in the winter of 1999 was done, it showed that only two were actively infected.

One of the great obstacles in the controversy is leaving jurisdiction of wild bison in Montana to the Department of Livestock rather than transferring it back to the Department of Fish, Wildlife & Parks (where it resided until 1995), the agency responsible for wildlife. (A bill to do just that was shot down in March 1999 in the Montana legislature.) For wildlife to be dealt with by the agency charged with overseeing domestic livestock is a travesty; a kind of final triumph of the nineteenth-century U.S. government campaign to rid the West of buffalo. Killing buffalo that first time around was also a political act, one designed to starve Indians into submission; to get them off the land and onto reservations. With them out of the way, the government could offer Indian land to settlers and cattle.

We've come an odd full circle. In the eyes of the settler—the rancher—buffalo once again pose a threat to his family and his herds. Only this time the government has replaced the Indians as adversary in the fight over territory. This would actually be quite funny, if it were not so tragic to see so many people fighting over a land they all love. And if the buffalo were not the pawn in a game that has nothing to do with him.

A HARD SEASON

THE 940-foot-long, two-lane bridge spans a deep canyon of the Gardner River. From road to river, the drop is over 200 feet. I was halfway across, on my way from Mammoth to Lamar Valley, when a big bull buffalo started down the center from the far side. Squeezing by the 1,800-pound, six-foot-tall animal did not seem an option. I stopped my vehicle. He never paused. I shifted into reverse and backed off the bridge, trying not to look down. The buffalo stayed on the road to Mammoth. Turning, I (discreetly) followed.

This is a hard winter. An ice crust formed beneath the snow has kept buffalo and other ungulates from reaching grass. Many have left their usual winter range in search of food.

My buffalo stopped at Rescue Creek, a few miles north of Mammoth. Lowering his huge head, he plowed snow aside. Pawing the ground, he found only ice. Near Yellowstone's north entrance at Gardiner, he headed up the valley west of the Yellowstone River, as if some old knowledge led him north. In the Gardiner schoolyard he scrounged a bit of scraggly grass at the edge of the running track where the feet of children had worn snow and ice to earth. The grass was not much, but it was more than anything else had been.

I stopped to watch him, then drove 2½ miles farther north to the park's Stephens Creek facility, where the park had arranged a media opportunity for journalists interested in buffalo. A ranger met vehicles at the locked gate through which one must pass to reach Stephens Creek. This is where park horses and vehicles are kept. There are several horse corrals and a long, neat row of vehicles. And now, corrals specially built to hold buffalo. These are lined with huge sheets of plywood so that daylight does not show through the rails. The buffalo remain somewhat calmer if they cannot see daylight ahead of them. Catwalks built about 8 feet up the outside of the corrals provide rangers a place to stand to do whatever controlling of the buffalo they must do.

For weeks buffalo had funneled along a drift fence into the buffalo corrals, where they were sorted into separate pens according to sex and age, then urged down a narrow corridor into waiting horse trailers that would haul them to slaughterhouses.

For two days prior to my arrival, a vet from the federal Animal and Plant Health Inspection Service had been testing captured bison for brucellosis. Until the APHIS vet arrived, *all* buffalo captured here were shipped to slaughter. After the testing, it was decided to hold those testing negative, and send only those testing positive. Unfortunately, the testing itself proved deadly. The buffalo, terrified at finding themselves trapped and surrounded by shouting people, fought to free themselves. Four were so badly injured they had to be shot. The park decided to end the testing.

I watched a group of cow bison fight the route down the narrow corridor to the waiting trailer. They fought piling into the trailer, but there was no way out. They piled on top of one another. The rangers slammed the trailer door shut, several pushing against it to hold it closed, while others chained and locked it. The trailer pulled away. The bulls destined for the next trailer refused to enter the corridor. "Whooo! whoo!" the rangers shouted. "Aye! Aye! Aye!" they shouted, banging paddles and shovels against the sides of the corrals until, finally, the bulls, too, piled into the trailer on their way to death.

The day I watched was the last the park shipped buffalo to slaughter. Park rangers were sickened by the trapping. You could see it on the faces of those at the buffalo corrals, even as they shouted and banged their paddles. When the last of three horse trailers loaded with buffalo took off for the slaughterhouse, the chief ranger said, "This is a real travesty." North district ranger Mona Divine told me, "We don't want them in here. We hazed 120 last night. Some of those are down near the north entrance. Some the state is shooting now."

We could hear the crack of rifles less than 2 miles up the road. "They refused our offer of help to haze them back to the park," Mona said.

Although it is not particularly easy to move bison someplace they don't want to go, hazing—pushing them in a particular direction by using noise, horses, helicopters, anything available that will get them moving—is a technique that sometimes works.

I drove up the road, across the boundary between Yellowstone and land owned by the Church Universal and Triumphant, where the Department of Livestock was shooting buffalo. The road crosses sagebrush and grassland that back to the west into the foothills of the Gallatin Range, and to the east to the Yellowstone River. On the east side of the river, the land rises onto benches and cliffs and then up into the Absaroka Mountains. The past few days had been sunny, with little new snowfall, and there were areas along the road where sage rose out of the snow. The day was cold, brittle, sunny. Just before crossing the park boundary onto church land, I saw my old bull buffalo grazing in a small patch of sagebrush. "Stay where you are," I said to him.

By the time I reached the fields where more than 16 buffalo had been shot, the shooters were at rest while several men gutted and skinned the dead buffalo. A man I knew had told me he would be in the field dressing out buffalo on this day, but I did not see him. The DOL calls in private citizens, mostly Indians, who pay their own way but keep the meat, heads, and hides to dispose of privately.

Because this meat has not been inspected by a USDA inspector, it cannot be sold publicly. The meat butchered at most of the slaughterhouses to which the buffalo have been taken is inspected and is sold at public auction. If a shooter from the Montana Department of Fish, Wildlife & Parks is called in to make a kill, that animal is sold at their own auction, along with any confiscated animals, such as illegally shot elk or deer.

Sun glittered on the neat, shiny mound of gut piled in front of each carcass. Two DOL trucks were parked in the first field. From the road, I watched the men working on the buffalo. So did two men from a Billings television station, here to get the story of the buffalo killing for the daily news. We were not invited onto the private land although, after 40 minutes, I walked into the field to ask the DOL whether I might watch the butchering close up. I wasn't sure why I wanted to do that, but it somehow felt necessary to watch the whole process; in some way to bear witness.

"If you wait a little, they're taking eight more down the road and those will be *on* the road, and you won't have to go on private property. Ma'am," the man said.

"How will I know when to go?" I asked.

"Just follow us when we leave," he said.

I waited half an hour. Nobody moved. The men field-dressing the fallen buffalo had finished their work and loaded the carcasses onto trucks. Nothing at all was happening in the field. I suddenly felt that nothing at all ever would, or that nothing ever would until the next group of animals had been shot (or, as the man said, "taken"). I decided to drive up the road on my own. So did a park photographer and the two TV reporters from Billings.

We all parked across the road from the eight buffalo. They lay resting at the far edge of the field, as they have for 10,000 years. "You will die soon," I said to them, but they did not hear. After a while, one animal stood and began its meager grazing.

We waited another half hour, but no DOL trucks appeared. An old red truck I had seen at the first field drove past. Over the radio scanner in the TV reporters' van we heard a man say, "They're bedded down out here. Everything's quiet." The truck pulled off the road below the buffalo. The radio was silent a moment, then a man said, "I don't want to go up there while those TV guys are hanging around."

"I'd like to see them in a ditch," a second voice said.

"The river would be better," the first voice said.

The next words over the radio were those of one of the DOL agents announcing that they were going to lunch while we remained parked in front of the buffalo. What I do not understand is that, since the shooting is perfectly legal under the interim bison management plan (the plan in place until a permanent method for dealing with buffalo is adopted), however one may feel about it, why are they so secretive? True, shooting a buffalo on the evening news is not great press, but goodwill gestures can always be used to anyone's advantage. The DOL doesn't need to come off as villains. Yet they persist. They had refused the morning's offer by the rangers at Stephens Creek to help haze the buffalo back into the park. Why, I wondered.

The Billings TV crew, the park photographer, and I also decided to go to lunch. I left last, driving back, past the first fields, past the park boundary. My old bull hadn't moved from his spot on the park side of the boundary. "Don't move," I said. "Don't move north. Please don't move north."

It took 20 minutes to buy a cup of tea in town and drive back out to the fields. The buffalo had moved a few yards north. He stood now just over the boundary, on church land. "Move back," I said. "A few feet. Move back."

There was one truck in the first field. All the carcasses and the skins had been removed from both fields, which were now empty but for shimmering masses of gut piled here and there on the white snow. I walked over to the truck to ask if they had seen the man I knew. The agent I spoke with looked relieved. "We thought you were from PETA," he said. PETA (People for the Ethical Treatment of Animals) is among the animal rights groups protesting the buffalo slaughter. The DOL does not like them. "No," I said, "although I'm surprised no one is here. I just want to write a story about this whole process."

"There should be people down at the other field soon," the man said.

I drove back down to the field of eight buffalo. They had moved uphill and were virtually hidden in tall sage and juniper. I could see only two. There were no other vehicles around. I sipped my tea and watched them through binoculars. Two trucks drove up, crossed the field without stopping, and headed into the sage. A man climbed out of each. One disappeared into the brush. I heard the crack of a rifle.

Again and again. The second man walked straight ahead from his truck, shouldering his rifle just as one buffalo lowered his head to graze. I heard a shot. The buffalo walked clear of the sage; away from the shooters. The man aimed toward him and shot again. The buffalo kept walking. They're letting him go, I thought. The buffalo fell.

The TV crew missed the shooting.

The shooters drove back across the field and parked at its edge. Several other trucks appeared. From nowhere. They stopped at the entrance to the field and spoke with the shooters. I walked toward them as a man in blood-stained yellow rain pants walked toward me. "You can go in with me," he said to me. "I'll ride in your vehicle."

As we drove across the slick, rutted snow, Bill LaFromboise asked if I intended to take pictures.

"I just write," I said.

"What do you want to know?" he asked.

"What happens to a buffalo. I want to see what happens."

We left my vehicle in a field of sage where eight dead buffalo lay. The sweet scent of sage, floating like a blessing about the buffalo, filled the clear, cold air. A little stream ran through the field. So these buffalo can drink, I thought.

"I don't want to see them all killed," Bill said, "but what are you going to do . . . ?" He dug his sharp knife into the thick fur at the buffalo's neck. Two other men worked with him. As they worked, we heard a shot. Looking up, we saw smoke.

"What the hell was that?" one man asked.

"I see lots of smoke over there," Bill said, pointing to an uphill clearing behind a stand of trees. "They must be using black powder," he joked.

I saw six buffalo on the hill a few hundred yards away. "They must be trying to scare them," Bill suggested. The buffalo continued looking for food, as if these lying around us were not dead. Then, suddenly, they moved off, down the back of the hill, out of our sight.

The men hooked the buffalo in front of me to a truck to move him into a better position to be worked on. As he was moved, I heard more shots, then realized the shooters just wanted to get the six on the hill out of sight to kill. Killing buffalo is something you want to do in private, apparently, like sex or gluttony.

The buffalo unhooked, Bill, with quick skill, cut neatly up the center of the animal's belly, opening the flesh. A big, shimmering ball of guts popped out.

"They're a fantastic animal," he said, pausing in what seemed a moment of homage. He punctured the gut bag, deflating it, then pulled it free of the animal.

As the bull's throat was cut, blood spilled out like a waterfall. A red pool formed in the white snow. Steam poured from his throat; the warmth of the animal's life entering the cold afternoon. Looking at his teeth, Bill said, "This one is six or seven years old."

Bill LaFromboise was not apologetic about the job he was doing. He is rightfully proud of his skill, carefully explaining to me the things he was doing. Respectful of the animal, he worked quickly and neatly. I am aware this animal is dead. I am not horrified by its death, although I am by its killing.

I left while men across the field continued their work on the fallen buffalo. The snow was dotted with red blood. Wherever you looked, there was blood. On the way to my vehicle, I passed the buffalo I watched fall. He was large and beautiful. No one had begun work on him yet. There were bubbles in his nostrils, the end of breath. I stopped to touch him, to ask his forgiveness. The fur on his head was so thick, my hand could not go all the way into it without pushing.

I drove back toward Gardiner, passing my solitary buffalo. Dead, he lay where I had last seen him, a few feet on the wrong side of the park border.

BUFFALO RANCH

LYLE Gunderson grew up on a South Dakota ranch. When he and Sharon married in 1956, they set up their own ranch 8 miles from the nearest road. It seemed remote to the close-knit people in this far-flung region. They worried about the Gunderson boy moving so far away. But Lyle saw it as space, not distance. His vision of the landscape stretched back to a time before the ranchers came. From childhood, he imagined buffalo grazing on this prairie. In 1972 he got some on his land.

"I got them to run much like as they were," Lyle told me soon after I arrived at the ranch to learn something about buffalo ranching for an article I was writing in 1992. "Lots of people ear-tag them and, some places, they're trying to get them registered. I bought 'em so I could run 'em like they were, so the less I can do with them, the better it is."

The Gundersons' white frame ranch house sits at the end of 8 miles of dirt road Lyle bulldozed across the prairie. Chinese elms shade the house from the insistent prairie sun. Birds twitter among the leaves. Two dogs lie in the trees' shade. There are tubs of red petunias in front of the house and three buffalo skulls leaning against the white wood fence surrounding the yard.

The walls of the pleasant, comfortable living room are hung with the heads of Lyle's hunting trophies, animals hunted on his own property. A buffalo robe lies over the sofa. A glass-doored case near the stairway is filled with rodeo prizes won by the Gunderson daughters, Deb and Susan.

Deb and her husband, Kevin Ploszaj, work the ranch with Lyle and Sharon. Susan and her family live nearby.

Lyle and I climbed up into his huge John Deere 535 baler out in the field where he'd left off work the day before. The enclosed, air-conditioned tractor had an inordinate number of dials, buttons, levers, and switches. Lyle carefully explained how they all worked. I thought mostly about how the thing cost more than my house.

Oats, barley, and speltz are all grown on the ranch. Harvested, they are rolled into huge round cylinders by the baler pulled by the tractor. Lyle manipulated various levers to make a finished bale come out even. You have to look backward to see what the baler is doing and forward to see where the tractor is going. You have to do both these things at once. Lyle made it look smooth. Easy. "You drive," he said. "Make a bale."

I tried to tell him his tractor was too expensive for me to drive, but I guess a man who has brought up two daughters on a ranch doesn't know about excuses. So I drove. I made a bale. I have a photo of me with my bale. It's a little narrower on one end.

The Gundersons ranch cattle and sheep as well as buffalo, a hedge against market variations. "Ninety percent of the time, when cows are down, sheep are up," Lyle said. "There's always somebody calling, all year long, for buffalo meat."

Buffalo has staying power. When ranchers lose cows and sheep because they drift with the storms, buffalo face right into them and survive. In a hard winter, when cattle must be fed, bison can manage on their own, pushing aside the snow with their huge heads to get down to grass, or with half the feed cattle need. There is a reason buffalo were so successful on the prairie.

Lyle and Sharon and I climbed into his truck to drive out to look at buffalo. We crossed miles of prairie. Cactus was in bloom everywhere, its delicate, tissuelike flowers—orange buds and lemon silk blossoms—laying low color across a dusty, muted earth. The land smelled of sage. Wind pressed gently through the grasses and blew the green-gray sage into silver. As the truck approached the buffalo, most of the new babies, as red as flowers—their fur darkens after their first summer—ran to their mothers. The mothers, ragged with shedding, their thick winter coats tattered by the changing season so that tufts of fur hung oddly here and there, snorted to the slower calves to come. When Lyle stopped the truck, we all got out.

"Don't turn your back on them," Lyle said.

Sharon threw cakes to the buffalo (cubes of pressed barley). The buffalo, which regard these as supreme treats, surrounded the truck, circling in closer and closer, always watching us as they picked up the cakes from the ground, their great, huge, dark eyes locking us into the center. I was aware of the truck at our backs. Among the animals, one caught my eye. He was gorgeous. Of all the adult herd, he alone had an intact coat.

"That's Bob," Lyle said. "His tail is bobbed—maybe froze off. He's about shed off."

I fell instantly in love with Bob. Falling in love with an animal is much like falling in love with a person. It causes you to make assumptions that a relationship exists. Sometimes you're actually right. Other times, it is all in your imagination. Either way, it makes for intense moments in the beloved's presence. Your perceptions are heightened. All your senses are alert. Whether or not the buffalo (or the horse or the cat or the boa constrictor or the person) returns your affection is irrelevant. What matters is how much more you notice.

I noticed Bob's perfect head, the full chaps of dark fur covering his front legs, the thick cape falling back from his head over his hump and shoulders. I noticed the chocolate brown color that was as deep as the earth. Where the sun hit, there was a reddish glow along his hump and down his backbone. The thick fur on his head and beard and front legs was almost black, like the earth taken up and molded into animal form.

But all the buffalo are like the earth.

I have a Navajo mud-toy, a deep brown buffalo. Made of earth, it holds the spirit of the buffalo and the spirit of the earth. Ten thousand years old, this buffalo knows things we cannot approach. It knows that all things come and go. I suppose it doesn't really care. Or not care.

Bob stood close to us. His horns were worn at the sides from rubbing them on the ground as he rolled in the dust. I saw the softness of those huge, dark eyes we cannot understand.

When Sharon and Lyle saw how enamored I was of Bob, they suggested I move away from the truck—a little— for a *quick* photo with Bob behind me. I have this photo, too. We look pretty good together.

The herd milled around the truck until the cakes were gone, when they moved a short way out to continue grazing. Their soft snorts mixed with the sound of their hooves on the dry earth; the slight breeze. Their snorts and snuffs sounded like the wind; their presence on this prairie is as natural as wind. A baby lay down on a mound of dusty earth and almost rolled. His mother went to him, stood over him, licked him, walked away. We climbed back into the truck. The buffalo moved past us, watching. We were inside the herd.

Caking these animals was not just for my benefit, but is an important control measure. "They'll come right to you because we cake them," Lyle told me. "Then, if you've got enough power," he continued, meaning enough trucks or horses and people, "and the country's smooth enough, you can move them."

I thought of all I'd been told about how difficult it is in Yellowstone to get the buffalo to go where rangers want them to go. "When they don't want to go someplace," Lyle added, "it's awful close to impossible to get them to go there.

"They're tough to handle—you've got to have good corrals," he continued. "If they can see through them, they'll make a hole or beat their heads against it and kill themselves."

The corrals are 7 feet high and solid wood. Although they have been built to contain buffalo, the same corrals are used to work both sheep and cattle. Planks nailed across the walls about 2½ feet up from the ground serve as an escape hatch in case a buffalo charges someone in the corral. You can jump onto the plank to launch yourself the rest of the way up and over. You do, however, need to move fast.

The buffalo get worked twice a year. Two-year-old bulls are brought in for butchering about the end of October; the cows and calves in early January when the calves are weaned. Once separated from the calves, the cows grunt their good-byes through the fence. When the corral is opened, they take off and never look back. (Domestic cows would try to get back into the corral to get their calves.) The calves are vaccinated against brucellosis and the heifers are branded.

The gathering of the buffalo is done with trucks. Because the buffalo associate the trucks with cake, they are likely to follow them. "We used to chase them on horseback," Sharon said. "That got *real* western, I can tell you . . ."

"There's a children's rodeo tonight," Deb said to me. "My sister's children are competing, so we're all going. You're welcome to join us if you'd like," she added, cautiously, so that I understood she thought I might be one of those people who disapprove of rodeo. "I love rodeo," I said.

Perhaps the only sport that comes out of the real work of real people, rodeo is an extraordinary tribute to the skill of the cowboy or cowgirl and to the spirit of the horse. To recognize the skill of the working person—in this case, a guy who spends much of his working life in cowshit—to sanctify it with ritual and costume, not to mention prize money, is something our society does not commonly do. I like it that rodeo recognizes that skill.

As we drove the 20 miles to town, Deb asked me what sort of article I planned to write.

"I don't really know, yet," I said. "I rarely know until I see what my story is."

"Tell her why you're asking," Sharon said.

"Some TV people came out to do a story," she said. "We invited them into our homes and showed them our community. We thought they wanted to do a story about ranch life here. But when we saw the show on television, and saw what they had done, we just felt used. They had used us for their own story."

"We have a new church," Sharon said. "We're all very proud of it. We took them to it, but on the show they just used the old church. It makes us look poor."

"I wish I had seen it," I said.

"We have a copy," Sharon said.

They hadn't trusted me, as a journalist, but had invited me in anyway. I was awed by their generosity of heart.

The rodeo grounds were filled with three-year-old boys wearing black jeans and cowboy boots and cowboy shirts and hats, looking serious and focused—the same serious, focused expressions I see on cowboys at the College National Finals Rodeo, or at professional rodeos. They practiced roping an iron horse's head or an overturned can. Slightly older children exercised their horses outside the arena. The two sets of bleachers were loaded with women holding babies, with fathers, brothers, and sisters. A horse stood between the bleachers as if he were a spectator. A dog, cruising the arena, stopped to investigate a puppy on a lead. There were small cowboys on horses; slightly larger cowboys on horses; little cowgirls; pretty cowgirls with long hair and colored jeans; ropes being twirled everywhere. I watched a mother tie the rope on a boy's saddle horn for the breakaway roping and realized that every parent in the stands had probably competed in rodeo. The wind came up. The low sun, hot during the day, dropped behind clouds. The arena dust blew into the stands. A boy came out of the chute on a horse like a tornado. He threw his rope true, landed his calf fast.

The families in the bleachers cheered each kid. Everybody here was a hero. No one was out to kill the opponents. There were no opponents. The test is only one of individual skill, a way to measure where one is. For these children it is one route to pride in who they are.

In the morning cool, Lyle and Kevin pushed Lyle's red and white 150 Super Cub out of its hangar. Lyle flies over his land at least once a day to check on herds, fences, waterlines, pastures. He invited me to go with him. I'm not fond of flying (besides, by this time I had driven the tractor, operated the baler, driven the truck, run a four-wheeler across the pastures, ridden a horse, and milked a cow and I was afraid he'd suggest *I* take the controls). But I was not about to pass up the trip. Flying ninety miles per hour at about 1,000 feet, we covered an area of about ten square miles. The patterns were fascinating—buffalo here, sheep there, cattle, more buffalo, antelope between them all as if these swift creatures of the prairie tied everything together—the intertwining of grassland and badlands; the Little Missouri with its low, muddy water striping through mud; the green fields of oats and barley and speltz. I recognized the field where I drove the tractor the day before; the tractor again parked where the day's work ended. We cruised over the site where a triceratops was being excavated. I added dinosaurs to the list of buffalo, sheep, cows, and antelope on Lyle's land. Ranching through the eons.

Lyle checked his water tanks. He had dug wells in the corner of four pastures, then dredged a six-foot ditch to run water out to all four pastures, a more economical construction than using electricity to pump water into every pasture. He noted where there was a fence to fix; where some cows had gotten out. He must have seen a hundred things I didn't even know were down there. By the time he brought the plane back down—without having suggested I fly it—I had a sense of the immensity of this world, of the connections here among animals, water, sky, and earth. Kind of a God's-eye view—close enough for intimacy; far enough for perspective.

With Sharon and Deb, I watched the tape of the television show that had so distressed them. Their distress was justified. The crew had presented the Dakota prairie as a wasteland, where people's lives were too hard and too lost; where attempts to build fell to ruin. The show's bias was one that espoused the idea of a Buffalo Commons across the Great Plains as a necessity because, as we viewers could plainly see, there was nothing out here except the hopelessness that drives people from home.

The plains people interpreted the idea of the Buffalo Commons to mean they would be moved off the land to make room for a sort of vast national park where buffalo could roam freely. To people making livings on land their families had worked for several generations, this did not sit well. It did not account for the fact that there are people thriving here; that there are young families whose children compete in rodeo and grow up to become champions; that there are multigeneration families working the land successfully and with pride; that there are new churches built; new ranching techniques embraced; new dreams realized.

But the idea had erupted like a great volcano beneath the plains, seething and spouting and shaking the earth. The shock waves vibrated all the way back to New Jersey, jolting urban planners Frank and Deborah Popper, who had invented the phrase, about as much as they did farmers and ranchers on the plains. In 1987, the Poppers published an article in a professional journal exploring the boom-and-bust past, and prospects for the future, of the Great Plains. They had suggested a large-scale land restoration project called the Buffalo Commons. Academics (Frank teaches at Rutgers, Deborah at the College of Staten Island/CUNY), they figured only academics would ever see the article. They never dreamed all hell would break loose.

But it was a story for the media to love. It had everything. Farmers versus Buffalo. Sodbusting versus Wildland. Poverty versus Nature. Failure versus Success. History versus the Present. Guilt versus Redemption. The romance of the Great Plains, or the *idea* of the Great Plains, stirs the American imagination. The region has a mythic quality, like the steppes of Russia. Something vast, eternal, isolated, enigmatic; qualities irresistible to the press, especially if they can be mixed with poverty and hardship. Latching on to the concept of a Buffalo Commons, the media set out to offer proof the Great Plains was a destitute, failed place in need of being taken over by the government.

Indeed, the plains was losing population, as it had twice before, after each of two separate eras of homesteading had ended in drought and dust and exodus out of the region. But *some* people had stayed on the land. And made it. And they were irate at this onslaught by the media. By *Easterners*. *They* knew they were not a myth. *They* knew how to live in their own country. The Poppers, giving talks in the region to explain what they were actually saying, were greeted with deep anger. Armed guards became a necessity in the halls where they spoke. In Montana a talk was canceled because of a death threat.

This anger does not seem odd to me, considering the television show I watched with Sharon and Deb. The footage featured shots, such as one used twice, of a piece of loose metal siding moving slightly in the wind; of abandoned vehicles; of lean and weathered men wearing old jackets; shots guaranteed to produce an image of poverty. People who had worked hard, and intelligently, to make good lives for themselves were furious.

Almost a decade later, I spoke with the show's producer, Sam Hurst. "Basically, I went up there to look at a place that was losing population," he said. "What we went to examine, we found to be true."

Time is an interesting thing. Like a river, it offers us a flow that always looks familiar, but is never the same. Twelve years have passed since the Poppers published their research article. In this time, many of the people living on the Great Plains have come to understand the Poppers' thoughts differently. In January 1999, they were invited to Fargo as keynote speakers for the annual meeting of North Dakota's Northwest Farm Managers Association. There were no armed guards, no death threats. Ten years earlier, Fargo's daily paper, *The Forum*, had denounced them in an editorial. Now their appearance, and their work, merited a major, front-page story. A sympathetic story. A story about how much public opinion had softened in a decade; a story about how much that the Poppers had said was true.

Frank Popper sent me a copy of a paper he and Deborah had submitted to the *Geographical Review* as I was writing this book. In it, they emphasize the idea of a Buffalo Commons as a regional metaphor, writing, "Some critics and supporters saw the Buffalo Commons as a formal plan that purposefully laid out the location of particular land uses, but it was inevitably never much more than a metaphor."

As metaphor, it has the power to elicit dreams, to invent the future, to provide for continued life on the plains. As metaphor, it does all those things the Gundersons have spent their lives doing. It is a huge metaphor. It pulls people into it; into the possibilities it offers; into the dreams. It pulled Sam Hurst into it. Sam Hurst gave up producing television shows in Los Angeles. He became a buffalo rancher on the Dakota prairie.

ROCKY BOY'S BUFFALO

IT is a long way from the state road to tribal headquarters. Rocky Boy's is a small reservation—165,000 acres—but it didn't seem small as I drove across it; across rolling country covered by short brown grass where houses have been set down on the low places, grooves in the rolling earth; little subdivisions of government housing, the functional, boxy rectangles that have no connection with this land. The subdivisions never led to anything, any public buildings. They were just stuck out there in the landscape by themselves. Finally, convinced I must have made a wrong turn somewhere, I stopped to ask directions of an old man standing beside an old truck parked on the roadside. He was smoking a cigarette, having a moment to himself in a warm October sun. The third week in October, it was a hot afternoon.

"Am I on the right road to the tribal complex?" I asked.

"You took a long way," he said. "You have to go over that divide," he said, indicating some vague place among the distant hills.

Rocky Boy's Reservation is home to Chippewa and Cree. People of the buffalo, they came to Montana in the late nineteenth century, then spent years wandering without a home territory before the reservation was carved out of the old Fort Assiniboine military reserve in 1916. It was a small piece of land they were given. It remains small, although its size has increased since 1916. But so has its population.

Nestled at the foot of the Bear's Paw Mountains, its sere hills are pierced by rock outcroppings. An occasional dark stand of evergreens, shadowy, clings to rents in the hills. Starkly beautiful, it is a hard place, I thought as I drove. A dry place.

Beyond the divide, the road curved and descended and climbed through a landscape of steep hills and rocks and forest. Wherever these buildings are, I thought, they are well protected from the outside world. No idle passerby would ever find them. I came upon them suddenly, hidden by the hills in a little cul-de-sac. The road twists among the buildings so there is no straight line from anywhere to anywhere. Stopping where the road would let me off, I found myself at the Stone Child College entrance. Over the entrance there is a painting of buffalo under what seems a magic rainbow held by an Indian. I took the Indian to be a healer. I asked directions to the Department of Fish, Wildlife & Parks. The man I asked pointed out a building on the far side of the road. It still took me a few circles to figure out how to get there and I arrived 10 minutes late for my appointment with Don Meyers, the department's Game Warden Supervisor.

Don stood talking to several people in the central part of the building. He looked at me, then pointed at the clock. I thought he was admonishing me for being late, which seemed a singularly un-Indian thing to do. When I asked him about it later, he said he was simply inquiring if I was his one o'clock appointment.

What did I want to know, he asked as we entered his handsome office. A stuffed lynx on a high shelf in a corner behind his desk looked down on us, ready to pounce. "About buffalo," I said.

Several months earlier, at a buffalo EIS hearing in Billings, I had heard Don Meyers speak. Moved by his words, I called him later to see if I could come to the reservation to talk with him. His job included managing the tribal buffalo. I wanted to know how a man like that managed buffalo.

He suggested we go for a ride. I assumed it was to see buffalo. We climbed into a big, shiny pickup. A tape played Indian music, the soft, deep voices of the singers entering the truck cab like the wind's heartbeat. We drove up, away from the tribal complex. "This is where the herd used to be," he said, gesturing to one side of the road. It was hilly there, and forested, at least near the road. It seemed an unlikely place for buffalo and I thought I must have missed something. When we came to open fields, country that seemed much more likely for buffalo, there were, instead, the frames of lodges erected for past Sun Dances. Several cows lay near one of them. Not buffalo. Domestic cows. Don left the highway and drove onto the Sun Dance grounds.

The Sun Dance is one of the most vital and sacred rituals of the plains tribes. Because it contains enormous power, it was denied the tribes in the last quarter of the 19th century. First the U.S. government made it illegal, and then Christian missionaries who held sway on the reservations divided up among the various denominations made it immoral. The buffalo and the Sun Dance were taken from Indian people at the same time. The resurgence of the Sun Dance in the twentieth century was integral to the tribes' long fight to regain their own spirituality; their own culture. The two are not separate.

Bright-colored scarves, offerings, tied to the lodgepoles forming the frames, waved in the breeze. Scattered beyond the most recent of the lodges, old center poles— the core of the Sun Dance lodge circle—stood alone on the plain.

Don stopped the truck. He made no move to get out. We sat there, just looking at the lodgepoles rising against the sky, echoing the shape of mountains in the distance behind them. Don's father is a Sun Dance chief, one of only two left on the reservation. His grandfather and his uncles were Sun Dance leaders as well. The Sun Dance ceremony at Rocky Boy's owes its existence to people like these men, the elders who believe in the necessity of the sacred celebration, and insist upon its presence in their lives.

The first Sun Dance at Rocky Boy's was held in 1918. The ceremony had to be modified because there were no buffalo skulls anywhere. Not only did buffalo no longer roam the plains, but their bones—their skulls—were also gone, gathered by destitute farmers to sell to glue factories for income enough to hang on a little longer. Or to move on. Farming a dry land had failed. They scoured the plains for bones. And then the bones were as gone as the buffalo.

"Everything was taken away from the plains after the slaughters," Don said. "We couldn't find no buffalo skull. We ended up using a steer skull.

"Which might not seem significant to a non-Indian," he added.

In a way, it would be like offering communion with grape juice instead of wine in a Catholic church, or blowing a trumpet instead of a ram's horn on Rosh Hashanah in a Jewish synagogue. In another way, there is no comparison, because neither the Catholic nor the Jew sees the vine or the ram as a relative. For the Indian, the buffalo is kin.

The buffalo plays a central part in the Sun Dance ceremony. His skull is kept inside the lodge, out of sight, while the dancers, who neither eat nor drink for the three days and nights they spend praying and dancing, move toward a dreamlike state in which they may have a vision of the buffalo alive, charging. The buffalo gives his power to the dancer.

A buffalo skull was presented to Rocky Boy's by the Blackfeet. Although it lacked the tradition surrounding a skull used in the Sun Dance—in which the person sponsoring the ceremony participates in a prayerful way in the killing of the buffalo, then prepares it for the event—it was a welcome gift.

"People say that we worship the buffalo," Don said. "We don't worship the buffalo. We respect it as God's creation. They're an equal partner in this whole thing we call Creation. We celebrate with all Creation at the Sun Dance ceremony. The buffalo is recognized as a symbolic leader of the four-legged—antelope, deer, elk—all these different four-legged beings. The buffalo represent that nation. They also play a part in our survival, as a kind of spokesperson for the human beings because we depend on the buffalo's flesh, on its robes, on its parts to survive. To survive in terms of physical survival; of spiritual survival."

We sat in the truck on the Sun Dance grounds a long time. It was a place of importance to Don, but it was also as if he were setting the stage for me. As if I needed to begin at the sacred in order to understand the buffalo. The music on the tape continued, the voices weaving in and out of the lodgepoles like the colors of scarves waving on the poles. I wondered what the songs were. The cows lying near the old pole did not move.

"Those values that we have that go along with the celebration of the Sun Dance are being left behind," Don said. "Or we're making too many modifications to them. It wasn't just any old buffalo. It had to be a buffalo bull."

We drove away from the Sun Dance grounds and back onto the paved road. A few miles later, Don pulled into a driveway near a couple of small buildings. A young dog bounded to the truck, excited at having visitors, wanting to play. Don got out of the truck to pick up a crowbar from a shed. I climbed out to talk to the dog. Don put the crowbar into the truck bed. Watching, I noticed a tied bunch of sweet-grass in the bed; only those two things in the back of the truck, the crowbar and the sweetgrass. The dog chased the truck as Don pulled out, back onto the paved road. "I wonder what he would do if he ever caught the truck?" Don asked.

"The important thing is that we still have our songs," he continued, when the dog gave up and turned back toward the driveway. "The buffalo are respected and men-tioned in our songs. These songs, from years ago, were handed to the Indian people from the buffalo spirit itself. We still sing these songs today. I'm proud we still do that. That power is still there. That spiritual power and that con-nection with the buffalo is still alive. It's still going."

Buffalo songs are used in the Sun Dance. These songs are sung only during the Sun Dance, or other special cere-monies. They are passed down through the generations, from those who have them to those who feel called to them. At 45, Don is concerned the younger generations no longer feel the same calls. While there remain traditional fami-lies—as his is—on the reservations, many have lost their cultural heritage. Don says the difference between tradi-tional and nontraditional life is the difference between real-ity and the shadow world.

"Which is reality?" I asked.

"The traditional aspect that we're raised with. Respect for life."

As we drove, I paid little attention to the landscape, so absolutely was I focused on Don. The passion in his speech commanded attention. It was what I had heard in Billings. There was so much more to hear now, at Rocky Boy's. Still, because some recess of my mind continued looking for the reservation's buffalo, the corner of my eye registered mountain, forest, tracts of dry prairie, a few settlements as we passed them, no buffalo.

The herd Don mentioned earlier, the one that used to be among the trees we passed soon after leaving the Fish & Wildlife office, had consisted of about 25 animals. Then, when brucellosis became a big issue in the state, the tribe, fearful of the disease, slaughtered them. It sounded like an act in which nobody did much thinking. It probably would not happen the same way today. Today they have only five buffalo. They are hoping for more. The five came from the Crow.

They have to be *somewhere*, I thought.

"Our people are pragmatic," Don said, "really practical in terms of buffalo, in terms of survival. We understand and respect the Creation. We understand and respect that buffalo have power like other beings. But we also believe that they were put here for a purpose, which was to help mankind, to help him survive; protect us; provide clothing for us. We, in turn, have to respect them, respect the responsibility they were given.

"I'm not a buffalo hugger by any means," he said, suddenly fearful, I thought, that I might see him in a wrong light. "I know that buffalo are a means of survival," he continued. "Their meat is good. It helps us live. That's the bottom line. I don't want some rancher thinking that I'm just another bleeding-heart liberal."

Then, almost as an afterthought, he said, "Buffalo are dangerous. They'll take you out in a hot second, you know. That's their power. Strong, powerful beings."

We turned off the paved road onto a dirt track, driving across land brown with autumn. Stands of leafless aspen dotted the hillsides. Along the track, brown grass grew in bunches. *Now*, I thought, we will see the buffalo.

The track climbed and switchbacked until, on a hill, Don stopped on a steep slant, just after a sharp corner. There was a sheer drop-off on the driver's side, a steep bank rising inches away on my side. Two men waited at a gate, standing just below another truck that faced downhill, directly toward us. It looked more perched than parked to me. The gate was a long iron bar bent in the middle. Don took the crowbar to the two men, then wrapped steel cable from the winch at the front of the truck around the bar. He moved to one side with a black object in his hand, a remote control of some sort. Every once in a while the truck jumped slightly forward. From the passenger seat I could see the drop-off on the driver's side. I wondered if he had engaged the brake. I wondered if I should get out of the truck. None of the three men was in a truck. I wished I was out of the truck. I was afraid to get out of the truck because a) there didn't seem anyplace to stand, except where the men were, and b) I thought it might reflect badly on Don. As in: She is afraid I don't know what I'm doing; or: She is butting into the business of men. When Don climbed in to move the truck slightly, I asked if there was something I could do. Maybe, I thought, it would be something requiring me to get out of the truck.

"Yeah, stay in the truck," he said.

I wondered if it was legitimate to say that I'm terrified in the truck, on the edge of this mountain, as Don operated that gadget and the truck kept moving. I'm sure if I'd been born in Montana instead of New York, I wouldn't feel this way. I'm sure I'd understand trucks better. The singing on the tape continued. The sky was cloudless. Stone ramparts topped the mountains opposite. Except for the buffalo, everything that belonged here was in place.

Returning to the truck, Don backed partway down the hill so that the truck could face forward and he could drive ahead.

"What are you doing?" I asked.

"Trying to straighten out the gate. Somebody must have rammed it. Why?" he paused, looking at me. "Are you scared or something?"

He stopped below the hill where the gate was, but in line with it, got out again, and attached the cable from this angle. When the best that could be done with the gate was done, we backtracked to the paved road. *Now*, I imagined, we would see buffalo.

Don began speaking as if he had not been interrupted by winching a gate straight. He is, apparently, not the sort of man to be distracted. "The U.S. should reverse its policy of the extermination of the tribes' main source of survival, which is the buffalo," he said, launching into an invective about the nineteenth-century policy of getting rid of buffalo in order to subdue Indians. "They were successful in doing that," he said, "but they were *too* successful. Not only did they bring Indian country to its knees, they also affected the ecological balance in the western plains. We're still feeling the effects of that because that bison is no longer there to do its part in that ecological balance. It's kind of like an ecological wreck that happened in the 1800s that we're still dealing with today."

"How could it be corrected, given the fact of all the cattle?" I asked, suddenly thinking that maybe Indians had answers ecologists had not yet discovered. They do, after all, have connections science remains reluctant to acknowledge.

"It can't be corrected," he said. "That's the sad part about it. You cannot go back in time and change that. When you speak in terms of affecting the ecological balance on a global scale, it's almost incomprehensible as to how you can fix that. It's like what we're currently dealing with in terms of global warming. It's like the holes in the ozone layer. Which is priority? Human life or our need for modern conveniences? All these things that we take for granted. We destroy not only the ozone, but we destroy ourselves."

When I asked whether having buffalo on the reservation would mitigate that in some way, Don suggested that the sight of buffalo, the sense of a culture intact they provide, could give people on the reservation the opportunity to "rekindle the spirit within themselves." But what happens then, he wondered. "Where are we going to take that energy to?" he asked. "Are we going to direct it back to the earth, or to some other direction that we didn't even anticipate? These are some of the issues many spiritual leaders—especially Native American spiritual leaders—have to consider when they're passing on a ceremony or a rite or a song to an individual."

He paused for an instant, thinking, still driving. Now I watched the tan fields pass by the window, still certain we would see buffalo.

"My mind keeps going back to, how do you talk to a rancher whose main livelihood is cattle?" he said, finally. "You've got this other being, this buffalo, that may pose a threat to their existence, their way of life. How do you make them understand that what you're dealing with is more than just an economic thing, but an ecological and a historical and a cultural thing? Have it make sense to them so that they can realize the importance of this whole aspect of this whole plan?"

I asked him if any ranchers present at the Billings EIS hearing spoke to him after he testified. I had wanted to speak to him then, but by the time I got out into the hall to find him, he was gone.

"None whatsoever," he said.

"You speak so easily to people," I said, thinking how openly he spoke to me as we drove.

"I'm always a nervous wreck when I get in front of people."

"You didn't seem so in Billings," I said.

"When you speak from the heart and your soul and you're thinking—my ancestors sacrificed themselves. They died to protect this tradition . . . you know . . ."

He was silent. I was watching him and thought he would continue and then realized there were tears in his eyes. Crying, he pushed through the silence with words again, but the words lay under his tears.

"I was raised by my grandparents," he said. "How do you talk to a person like a rancher who has so much hate, and so much misunderstanding about our people? How do you make him realize that we're human beings, you know, and that we're just a small part in this whole thing we call Creation? How do you talk to a human being who has no value of anything other than another human being? And even that is questionable?"

He was no longer fighting his tears, these tears for his grandparents, tears for the earth. Tears were rising in me, too. For his grandparents. For his pain. For the buffalo that represented, for him, everything that worked. For the buffalo I was not seeing. I fought my tears back. One of us was enough.

"I was filled with a lot of hate, a lot of mistrust. I've seen my grandparents abused by white people who hated them just because they were Indian. I remember my grandparents not going into a restaurant because the restaurant had a sign saying—no Indians or dogs allowed."

The silence in the truck now was palpable, like heavy air pressing on my heart. I asked him if he wanted to stop the truck. He shook his head no. Neither of us had any

Kleenex. He wiped at the tears with his hand. I watched, wishing I could disappear so that my presence would not embarrass him. I watched the openness of his heart and felt hurt to my soul by the things his grandparents endured. His tears were their dignity.

"You know," he said finally, "the grand thing about it was, my grandparents were the first to forgive. The enormous rage, you know . . . when I remember the things they had to put up with. Rage. And how do you talk to people who have no value of their own religion? All they see is money. All they see is material. Things. How do you get *to* 'em? How do you get through to 'em? How do you make 'em realize and understand and see how reasonable it is, and how human it is, to allow for other human beings . . . not just human beings, other *beings* on this planet who play an important part to this whole ecological balance?

"When we kill a buffalo, kill any being—an elk or a deer—we understand that balance is sacred. It's something we understand that the Creator gave to us. Gifts. Wonderful gifts. Powerful gifts. Just to indiscriminately destroy them, with no feeling, no ceremony, nothing. Just as an object. A material object that you put a value on, a dollar value. How do you put a dollar value on the breath you take each day, or the heartbeat that beats in your chest? How do you put a dollar value on that?

"These are the things that we try to get through to these ranchers, but"—his voice changed in imitation of the *biiiggg* rancher—'Well, by god, the bottom line is the dollar. My cow's gonna eat that grass . . .' "

His face was wet with tears now. I searched all my pockets for Kleenex, knowing there wasn't any, but thinking some might appear anyway. He looked in the glove compartment. "I usually carry some," he said. Then, in acceptance of what is, he added, "Tears are good."

"Tears are very good," I said.

"It gets rid of all that stuff that's in your body. Chemicals, toxins come out," he said.

"The earth knows when you cry for it," I said.

"Sometimes, you know, Ruth, it's hard for me to talk about things like this without getting emotional. But I really get emotional. I have strong emotions when I speak about things like that. A lot of people don't understand the connection, the power that there is today. It still exists with Indian people. And even with non-Indian people, for crying out loud! They just refuse to accept it."

There was a long silence then. Don continued driving. I watched the land go by. I felt helpless because I could not change history; not undo the pain, the loss, the absence of compassion. I can listen, but it isn't much. I can understand pain. My own people have been refused admittance to places. No Jews and no dogs allowed. But I have never seen it. I cannot know what Don knows.

"It just boggles my mind," he said as we returned to the Fish & Wildlife building, "that these old-timers had the bigness of heart to forgive at the drop of a hat. That goes back to traditional ways. To forgive."

"How does life go on, without being able to forgive?" I said.

49

"Maybe that's why they learned to forgive," Don said. "Because life goes on."

I left the reservation without having seen the five buffalo. I think seeing them had never been the point. What Don had done instead was take me to witness the absence of buffalo. What he showed me was the sacredness of buffalo.

CHIEF

JERRY Wayne Olson drives back and forth across America with his buffalo, Chief. They perform at rodeos and county fairs and in theaters much of the year. Jerry Wayne's wife, Judy, who travels with him and Chief and Dude, Jerry Wayne's horse—with whom he also does an act—sent me a schedule of their bookings. The closest town to me on their itinerary was Kalispell, where they were scheduled as the halftime act at the PRCA rodeo held nightly during the Northwest Montana Fair.

I knew only three days ahead of time I could get to Kalispell for the rodeo. Not much advance notice, but surely enough time to arrange a meeting with Jerry Wayne. I was eager to meet him; eager to see his buffalo. In 1989 I saw Jerry Wayne's father perform with *his* buffalo at the Livingston Roundup Rodeo. The enormity of trust between the man and his buffalo moved me to tears. Jerry

Wayne's father has since retired. Jerry Wayne looks just like him.

I was also eager to see something of this aspect of being a buffalo—being a performer—an aspect hugely different from that of buffalo in Yellowstone, or ranched buffalo, or the erstwhile buffalo on the plains. I thought it would help me understand further what being a buffalo means.

I called Jerry Wayne at home in Belle Fourche, South Dakota, to set up a meeting, but the Olsons were already on the road to Montana. I called the fair office to arrange a meeting. It seemed a simple enough thing. A woman named Cherie said, "You need to speak with Diane."

I called Diane, who did not call back. I called the next day with no more luck. I called the following morning, before starting my drive to Kalispell. Diane answered. "Oh, you need to speak with the rodeo liaison, Judy K," she said. "She can arrange things with the buffalo man."

I called the rodeo office three times, with no answer, then called Cherie back, asking her to arrange a meeting for me with Judy K about seven o'clock and have the woman leave a message at my motel about where to meet.

From Bozeman, where I live, it is 331 miles to Kalispell. Once you get past Missoula, Highway 93 takes you the rest of the way. Highway 93, which passes by Flathead Lake and through the Flathead Reservation, is lined with things buffalo. Stores sell buffalo jerky; restaurants sell buffalo burgers; the People's Center on the Flathead Reservation has a beautifully mounted exhibit on buffalo; the

National Bison Range at Moise has a few buffalo lying around in pens and many more in the hills. The Bison Range Visitor Center has its own bison exhibits and videos and literature. Not that it's very easy to stop at most of these places. Traffic on Highway 93 is bumper to bumper. It's like the Long Island Expressway on a July day. Flathead Lake. The Atlantic Ocean. Same thing. One just saltier than the other. If you get off the road to buy a buffalo burger, it can take 20 minutes to get back on.

The temperature was in the 90s. Occasional storms that cooled nothing slid down the road. In Kalispell a drenching storm had left small rivers at the curbs and ponds in all the low places of pavement. By 6:00 P.M., there was no message waiting for me at the motel. I drove out to the fairgrounds, where no signs indicated any parking at all. The ground was a gray, slick, thick mud.

I parked across the street in a supermarket parking lot where teenage boys were selling parking for $3 a car, then asked directions to the rodeo office at the entrance gate. The ticket seller assured me it was as far from the entrance as it was possible to be. I twisted my way through the crowds to the muddy midway. After walking a good distance, I encountered a blond woman on a large horse. The woman wore a red, white, and blue sequined cowboy shirt and a white cowboy hat. Her makeup was perfect. She and the horse both glittered. I figured *she* would know where the rodeo office was. "Oh, yes . . . it's this way," she said, pointing in the direction from which I had just come. At the end of the midway I came to a building marked FAIR OFFICE.

"Can I help you?" a squarish woman in a polyester pantsuit asked.

"I'm looking for Judy K," I said.

"She's in the rodeo office."

"I thought this was the rodeo office."

"This is the fair office. The rodeo office is down the midway, near the parking area."

"There are no signs for parking."

"Oh, it's so far away and very expensive."

"Anyway, I've already been down that way. A cowgirl told me to come here."

"But you have to go there."

"Can we phone?"

She hesitated a moment, as if using the phone when you could walk half a mile through mud never occurred to her, then pointed to the phone. It rang unanswered in the rodeo office. During this time, the woman walked away. But another one, older and kinder, appeared. "Can I help you?" she asked.

"I need to get to Jerry Wayne Olson," I said. "The man with the buffalo doing the halftime act. I was told I had to go through the rodeo office."

"Well, let me call," the woman said.

"I just did. There's no answer."

"Then let me see if I can find someone here who can help," she said, kindly, turning to a woman who had just walked in. "This woman needs to reach the rodeo office. She's trying to reach the man with the buffalo," she explained to the new woman, who already looked as if she'd had enough.

"Just tell me where I'll find him and I'll go there," I offered.

"Oh, no, you can't go back there unauthorized," she said, sighing with annoyance, as if she had been severely burdened by people who did not obey the rules. "I'll have to find Judy K. She's over there with the stock."

"I'll follow you," I said.

"That's not allowed," she said, sternly. "You wait here and I'll be back."

It was 7:45. The rodeo began at 8:00. I watched people come in and out to buy tickets for the next day's rodeo. A woman with a sick bull came in to call a vet. "He was all right this morning," she said, "but now he's just lying there puffing up. And just before the sale." I fidgeted. I watched the clock. I *knew* the woman would not come back.

A woman who had been busy at a desk suddenly noticed me. "What's happening?" she asked, walking over to me. The only person in the office who looked like someone I might know, she wore jeans and a denim shirt with a black velvet collar. She had long dark hair and a quiet sense about her.

"I need to find the buffalo man for a book I'm writing," I said, by now exasperated at the difficulty of doing something in a place—Montana—where things *used* to seem so straightforward. "I've just driven 331 miles to talk to him. I've spent three days trying to reach someone here so I could get to him."

"Why don't you just walk over there?" she asked.

"Because everybody says I can't."

"Just go through the gate, walk across the stands and back behind, and find him. It just . . ." She hesitated.

"Just what?"

"Just takes balls."

"I guess I can get them when I need them," I said, wondering when I had stopped doing things just because somebody told me I couldn't.

A man came out of an inner office. "What's the problem?" he asked. Denim explained to him. "I'll show you where you go," he said, taking balls for granted. We left the office. "Just go between those two buildings." He pointed beyond the ticket gate.

My boots slid into the slick mud. Mud oozed up over the bottoms of my jeans. Behind the bleachers, beautiful horses stood hitched to elaborate trailers parked on the grass. A few cowboys walked the muddy road. The loudspeaker blared the announcer's voice out of the arena, back here where cowboys and girls and handlers and horses all waited beneath the sound of his voice and the band playing and the storm-passed sky where gray clouds lined in gold piled up on top of rose-colored clouds. The announcer introduced the cowgirls who opened the rodeo. Even without seeing them, I knew they all wore sequins. I knew they all came loping into the arena, rode the railing around the arena waving their two-fingered, rodeo-queen wave, looking as glamorous as movie stars used to, but a lot stiffer. But they rode well. I asked a woman in a glittering purple vest if she had seen a buffalo somewhere back there. She pointed me toward the end of the road, toward the entrance to the arena. A few cowboys exercised horses on a large oval track behind the parked trucks and trailers. Dogs were tied underneath trucks. I looked everywhere for a buffalo. It didn't seem the sort of thing one could hide. Finally, the second pass through, I noticed a large, new truck from Belle Fourche, South Dakota, with a shiny silver trailer attached. There was nobody around. No buffalo.

Two cowboys in the trailer parked next to Belle Fourche were getting ready for their go-round. In front of the open door, one was putting on his jeans. I waited until he had his pants on, then walked toward them just as the other, not seeing me, came out spitting. At my feet. "Excuse me, Ma'am!" he said, almost bumping into me.

"Does this trailer belong to the buffalo man?" I asked, pointing.

"Knock on it and see," he suggested, having no idea at all what was next door to him. I figured he probably wouldn't win. Or maybe that was just the focus that it takes to win. Hard to know whether complete awareness takes away from focus or increases it.

I knocked. Jerry Wayne Olson came to the door, knotting a silk scarf around his neck. A big man with a round face, he seems the right type to be riding a buffalo. He and the buffalo are the right type for each other. Each seems as if he would be slow and ponderous, but each moves with real thought, lightning speed, and great agility. They each have the same kind of sweetness in their faces and their posture. A kind of eager hopefulness.

I introduced myself, wished him luck, made plans to return after the show, and walked back through mud to mud-smeared bleachers. Too late to get a reserved seat, I climbed up the bleachers to stand between sections. Some people had brought towels to wipe off their places. Others sat on rain jackets. I was wearing light blue jeans and a suede vest and was not about to sit anywhere. Standing, I had an overview of the broncs and the cowboys preparing themselves to ride, lowering themselves carefully onto the horses, wrapping tape around their hands to increase their grip, almost ready. The horses looked sturdy and healthy and, when they came out of the chute, they were flying, twisting, bucking, sunfishing pounds of high-test animal. There wasn't a cowboy here who could blame a low score on the animal. (Of course, I hate to admit this because the rodeo liaison who couldn't be bothered with me is from the family that provides the rodeo stock. But they've got some good animals.)

I watched the bronc riders and the bulldoggers and the bull riders. I saw the $50,000 Calgary Stampede bulldogging winner fail to drop his steer. I guess anybody can have an off night. I watched the bull riders warm up like some kind of oddly clothed exotic dancers. Deep bends from the waist to a flat back, one arm raised to make half circles in the air while the other hand is placed over the crotch, the fringe on fancy leather chaps shaking with all the moves like the feathers or veils of dancers.

While I watched, the sky darkened so that the flashing neon colors luring people to the fair rides beyond the rodeo arena could be as vividly seen by angels and extraterrestrials as by us in the bleachers. At night the gaudiness of the fair, all fairs, explodes into colors and lights and sounds and smells and movement that churn everything in its environs inside itself so that it all—the rides, the crowds, the bull riders in their fancy chaps—becomes one mass like the gases waiting to form the earth.

And then the man rode in on the big, dark buffalo.

There was a ripple of applause through the jammed stands and a kind of gasp you could feel in your gut. Dressed in a silky purple shirt and white pants, a white silk scarf knotted around his neck, the man looked natty. Sitting well back of the buffalo's hump, he held the long, heavy reins in one hand, his white hat, raised in greeting, in the other. "He comes out of the hills of South Dakota!" the announcer's voice bellowed over the speaker system as the buffalo trotted the circle of the arena like some archaic force of nature on its route through time.

Eyes straight forward, Chief circled the arena as if none of us were there; as if it were only him and the man on his back. Yet he knew. He could hear the applause. He could smell the human smells in the warm night. He could sense the heartbeats held in awe.

"Old Chief is working well tonight," the announcer said.

Chief walked a figure eight, then backed up at Jerry Wayne's command. Jerry Wayne jumped off to stand in front of the buffalo, facing him. Chief kneeled and walked forward on his knees. Jerry Wayne walked toward him and Chief walked backward on his knees.

"It's going to be a cold night in the Black Hills," the announcer said. "What do you do?"

Placing a blanket on the arena ground, Jerry Wayne lay down. Chief kneeled across him. "If Chief would just kneel the long way, you could take advantage of that warm buffalo robe with its heart beating," the announcer said. Chief changed position so that they both lay in the same direction, the man and the buffalo. The man caressed the buffalo's face. It seemed a moment of deep affection, a private moment. Then, grabbing Chief's horns, he pulled himself back to his feet. Standing, he turned his back to the buffalo. The buffalo did not move.

Judy Olson drove the truck pulling its long silver trailer into the arena. A metal ramp was lowered from the top of the trailer, about 12 feet up, to the ground. Chief ran up the ramp to the top of the trailer where, on command, he lay down. (In the course of training, Jerry Wayne feeds his buffalo on top of the trailer so they will find the climb, and the narrow trailer top, rewarding.) Jerry Wayne climbed to the top of the trailer, gave Chief another affectionate pat, then moved a pedestal into position. Chief, now standing, placed his front feet on the pedestal, then raised one foot. "In salute to Montana," the announcer said.

For a moment, nothing moved. There was no sound. There was only the buffalo standing on top of a trailer with his foot raised in salute. For a moment both announcer and audience let the silence, and the buffalo, be. Then the announcer said, "You need cooperation from a buffalo because you can't force a buffalo to do anything."

Jerry Wayne sat down on the pedestal. Behind him, Chief placed a front leg over his shoulder. In 1989, at the Livingston Roundup Rodeo, I saw Jerry Wayne's father and his buffalo do this, too. I wondered the same thing now as I had wondered then. How does the buffalo know how much the man can bear? How does the man know the buffalo will follow the rules? The stance is almost possessive on the part of the buffalo. Proprietary. This is *my* person. *I* have trained him.

Jerry Wayne held out his hat toward the audience and the audience responded with applause. But with a palpable wonder as well. This is not an ordinary trained animal act, but a relationship of deep trust that we have somehow come to witness. That Jerry Wayne is also a showman is almost incidental.

Remounted (Chief bent slightly so that Jerry Wayne could climb on), Jerry Wayne signaled Chief to turn a tight circle to the left, then to the right on top of the trailer before descending the ramp, trotting the arena periphery again and heading, finally, for the door at the back of the trailer. Jerry Wayne jumped off Chief's back at the exact instant Chief jumped into the trailer. Judy drove the trailer away while Jerry Wayne raised his hat to the audience and ran out of the arena to applause that rumbled like the footfalls of buffalo moving across the plains.

Jerry Wayne Olson is a third-generation buffalo train-
er. The first family buffalo was trained by his grandfather
because somebody bet him he couldn't do it. Old-timers
occasionally come up to Jerry Wayne after a show to say, "I
saw your granddad and his buffalo." His father trained *his*
first buffalo because his own daddy had. Jerry Wayne told
me that in 1989, when I saw him perform, his father was
recovering from a broken back, but wasn't about to let that
stop him. Jerry Wayne thought he'd break the chain. Maybe
it's how you rebel when you grow up in a family where the
men all train buffalo, but he just didn't want a buffalo. "I
never did like the buffalo when I was a kid," he said. "They
was work, you know." He did horse tricks—blasting into the
arena standing on two horses, one foot on one, one on the
other. He loved the crowd's roar.

But there was buffalo in his blood.

Nobody dealing with the current buffalo issues thinks
about performing buffalo. Why would they? When the
concern is with the continuing existence of wild buffalo, this
is an aberration; a footnote; beside the point.

Maybe. Isn't the point exactly the relationship of
humankind and buffalo? Isn't it an issue of trust? Isn't there
something to be learned from the trust between a man and
his buffalo? Trust is what the Olsons have to work with. It
is what I saw in the performance of Jerry Wayne's father. It
is what I saw in Kalispell between Jerry Wayne and Chief.

So what if a trained buffalo is a kind of aberration?
Performing is a kind of aberration, too. Relatively few people or animals do it. But because performers provide us a

kind of safe insight into our own actions and feelings, we applaud, we laugh, we cry. Release, despair, triumph—we own it all through the performance. It hardly matters whether the performer is a great actor, a great racehorse, or an extraordinary buffalo.

Once, in New York, at a small, one-ring circus, I watched a herd of horses run into the ring; run around and around the ring. No person was obviously present to control them. They just ran into the ring from the dark nether reaches of the planet; ran like wild horses on the plains. The only light anywhere was the spot over the ring where the horses ran so that they were all you could see. You were alone with a herd of wild horses, drawn into them as they ran and ran until you no longer remembered there were people on either side of you; no longer remembered anything except these horses coming out of the heart of the earth to run.

The heart of the earth, heart of the horse; the buffalo; the person. Heart is the ingredient in great performance. You can see the heart as if it were a thing like eyes or legs. Watch a sled dog running or a racehorse running. Watch a great trail horse on a steep, rough, long trail. The animal does what it does with every fiber of its being. It gives everything it has to give. You see them go and what you say is, "Look at the heart that animal has."

Chief is a performer to the core. Out in the pasture, he doesn't pay much attention to Jerry Wayne, but as soon as he sees the trailer being hooked up he's right there at the fence, eager to go. The audience matters. The arena matters. The *performance* matters.

After the performance I walked back across the mud behind the stands, between the parked trailers, past tethered horses and sleeping dogs. The arena lights did not reach back here. The neon did not reach. It was pitch black. I could just make out an occasional person as I walked up the muddy road to the Olsons' parking spot, arriving in time to watch Judy backing the trailer in. Chief looked out the window of the back door, then turned around to appear at the side door of the trailer, as if he wanted to understand exactly where he was going. Seven little girls in cowboy hats and fancy shirts came to the trailer. Buffalo groupies, although one, apparently, had no idea why she was there. Just going along with her friends. "It's the buffalo man!" one of the girls told her.

In the light of the trailer's living quarters, looking at him in awe, they asked Jerry Wayne for autographs. He gave them each signed photos. An adult couple came to the door for pictures, as awed as the little girls. I stood watching, glad he has fans because his performance is wonderful. The fans are a corroboration of the years of work he has put in; the consolation for the lack of roaring applause he remembers from his days of galloping into the arena standing on two horses at once. He misses that roar at his entrance now.

"When I first started working Chief I was suprised that there wasn't that roar of applause I used to get when I Roman rode," he told me.

"But there is a kind of a gasp," I offered. "It's as if everyone is holding their breath. As if it is so extraordinary to see a man come riding into the arena on a buffalo that they don't know what to do . . ."

Judy Olson came out from behind the truck and the two of them readied the pen outside the trailer (next to Dude's pen) where Chief gets hay and grain and spends the evening. Jerry Wayne walked Chief around the trailer into the pen. It was like anybody walking a horse back to the corral. But this isn't a horse. I moved a little more out of the way of the dark animal in the dark night.

Jerry Wayne and Judy live in the front of the trailer. Chief and Dude, each in his own compartment, live in the back. Jerry Wayne and I sat on the gray plush sofa in the Olsons' small living space. Judy pulled up a wastebasket for a stool. "People ask me how come he works some performances so slow and some so fast," Jerry Wayne said. "He's wise, he's smart, he's earned the right to do it his way. As they get older, they get wiser. They learn to watch. If you pay attention to what they're telling you, you know what they're thinking," he said. "I've learned a lot from Chief— even as far as working horses. I think if people took the time to listen—they don't take the time to learn—the buffalo is the teacher.

"He can look at me and tell me what kind of a mood he's in—you can tell when something is wrong. He reads me. Whatever mood *I'm* in, that's how Chief works."

It must be a translation of the buffalo's need to read the landscape, the mood of the herd, the arrival of danger. The responsiveness of any animal to a person must be an adaptation of a natural instinct.

The Olsons have been questioned by animal rightists who believe the buffalo should be only wild. While both Jerry Wayne and Judy are targets for them, Judy seems more affected by it. Maybe as a woman, or maybe, because she does not work directly with Chief, or Tatanka, the young buffalo Jerry Wayne is currently training, she seems more accessible. "People say, 'Chief should be in the wild,'" she said. "But he's an only child and he likes it that way. He's a pet in a lot of ways, but he's still a buffalo. I guess you'd say he's part of the family.

"Why do they do that?" Judy continued, earnestly, about the behavior of animal rightists.

For the Olsons, animal rightists are a peculiarity, a group of people who believe there is only one right way; who see only a single role for animals. But the Olsons know from their own experience that interaction between species is possible. If enough work goes into it. Enough patience. Enough time. Enough care. They cannot understand the vindictiveness of a view that purports to care for life but looks at only one aspect of it.

"Why do they do that?" she asked.

The question was one to which she gave much thought. I tried to say that I thought the idea of protecting animals against our ideas of dominance and superiority matters, but that in the extremes of that protection we can forget we continue to make ourselves superior. But what I said didn't make much sense to me. It was late, and I was tired. I wanted her to empathize with the people who see themselves as protectors of animals, yet to feel my own empathy with her and Jerry Wayne and Chief. I honor wild buffalo, but I also honor the Olsons' way of life because it, too, treats the animal with respect and love.

"It's the extremes on both sides that allow us to meet somewhere in the middle," I said. Why did I say this when I cannot bear the middle? Anarchy—that adamant refusal to ally oneself with any one side—matters. But anarchy cannot protect the buffalo from the fears of the stockgrowers' associations or the machinations of the U.S. government. And removing all semblance of order, it will not allow the Olsons to dream their buffalo.

It was really time to leave. Judy was as tired as I was. But every time I tried to say thank you and good-bye, Jerry Wayne had some new thought. His energy is huge. He is a buffalo who can travel miles across the prairies, head into the wind forever.

"He still has his wild instinct," Jerry Wayne said about Chief. "You respect him for being a wild animal," he said.

It was after midnight when I left the trailer. No one moved among the parked trailers and trucks. Someone had taken all the dogs away. The rodeo arena was deserted, the arena lights turned off, the ground strewn with go-cups and food wrappers. On the midway, the neon rides still turned terrifying loops while throngs of teenagers checked each other out. A million miles away, at the quiet trailer I had just left, the dark buffalo munched hay in his pen. He had done well.

HEARING

It's hard for you as a human being to say—what are these animals doing? What's their crime? They're trying to stay alive. We do the same thing. We're functioning organisms that are just trying to stay alive. Those buffalo are just going out to try and stay alive. Jerry Ryder, Yellowstone Park ranger

IT was a hot early afternoon on a late August day in 1998 when I arrived at the Billings Holiday Inn to attend a hearing on the draft bison Environmental Impact Statement. The hearing, one of 18 being held around the country, was an opportunity for anyone to voice an opinion on the alternatives for action proposed in the EIS. Written testimony was also accepted.

Billings is the biggest city in Montana. It has a busy hodgepodge of a downtown, refineries you can smell if the wind is wrong, art, culture, a vast stretch of suburbs. The Holiday Inn, just off the interstate into town, is isolated from all of this. It could be anywhere. Billings is probably as far from wildness as Chicago, but sitting on the crossroads between mountains and plains, it might serve as a symbol of compromise.

The notice of the hearing was in a pile of mail waiting when I had returned from Yellowstone a few days earlier. Since then, I had pondered whether or not to testify. If I value my role as observer, I ought not publicly testify. But sometimes I wonder whether that bit of ethics is just a cover-up for my intense shyness. And if I care as hugely as I believe I do that buffalo are being needlessly slaughtered while ranchers are forced into an unnecessary atmosphere of fear, don't I have some kind of obligation to testify? I inserted my written testimony between the pages of the thick EIS document. I'll figure out what to do later, I thought.

Whatever I decided, I would, at least, record the words I have recorded at every hearing and forum and symposium I have attended for close to 10 years. The words never change. The beliefs, the fears, the awful dilemma of buffalo versus cows does not change. Maybe 10 years is too short a time for change. The buffalo have been here for 10,000 years without changing.

In the profoundly polarized atmosphere surrounding the buffalo question I feel inundated by a cacophony of voices tumbling over one another, as if everyone is speaking at once. No one hears anything they do not already believe. Nobody's words ever change anybody's mind. Some people feel trapped by the words. A biologist in Yellowstone who has been studying buffalo for 30 years has become afraid to talk to the press. When I spoke to her on the phone she told me she had in front of her a list on which item 4 said, "Rest assured anything you say may be held against you or misquoted." She was tired, she said, of being a target. At hearings and other meetings, the religious fervor with which people speak sweeps believers along in a holy war where listening is heresy, compassion, apostasy.

One autumn afternoon on the Fort Belknap Reservation, I stood amid the tribal buffalo. In the broad, dry vastness of the day, I listened to the prairie sounds surrounding me. Buffalo snorts and snuffs and breaths; the shuffle of hooves on earth so dry it rises with each footfall in golden dust; the sudden whistle of a prairie dog; a quick, faint rush of wind formed a gentle sort of music. We could use a little music; something that weaves harmony from the dissonance of the polarized voices. What if we all *sang* together? Music is a compassionate art—taking a myriad of sounds and playing them into a fluid whole. The disparate voices could compose themselves into a symphony. Something that ends in triumph would be nice. Something Beethovian, perhaps, although I think they are more apt to make a country song where the hero rides off into the sunset, never looking back at the world collapsing behind him.

This is the only herd that's been in place for ten thousand years. All the citizens are being used to provide political fodder. The process of taking due process away from ranchers is the problem.

Brucellosis is not *the problem. There's been bad press out there and everyone is being tainted by it. Why is everything so hard in Montana?*

Steven Torbit, senior scientist for the National Wildlife Fund in Denver

In the battle over the fate of Yellowstone's buffalo, Montana's livestock interests—represented by the DOL and the Stockgrowers Association—stand in opposition to wildlife interests, represented by environmental organizations, animal rightists, businesses, Indians, and many private citizens in the region, across the country, and, as we have seen in the response to the EIS, around the world.

Endless meetings are held, protests launched, bills brought before the legislature. Buffalo activists take to the trenches and get arrested. Local newspapers list the numbers of dead buffalo. Government officials entrench themselves deeper and deeper.

We've managed this issue like a dogfight. You've got bureaucrats on both sides of the issue refusing to budge because budging looks like capitulation in an argument that's been waging for 30 years.

John Mundinger, former administrative officer with the Montana Department of Fish, Wildlife & Parks

If I were to testify, what could I say? That if we save buffalo, we save the world? That we do not know what we do to the web of life by interfering with its patterns? Could dinosaurs have imagined mammals? Flowers? What if they had flung back the meteors and changed the route of time?

This is not what I have written on the paper I've stuck into the EIS. I've been more practical there. Less honest.

I continue attending these things, thinking something new might happen. I wonder if I am the only person in Montana that naive. Still, with an EIS that has been years in the making now in hand, shouldn't there be the potential for something new?

An EIS presents a number of options for the management of whatever the thing is that necessitates the EIS. A preferred alternative is presented by the agency developing the document, but nothing can be implemented without public comment being accommodated. In this instance, all sides of the public were allied in their distaste for the preferred alternative. Virtually everybody who came to Billings came to testify against it.

The alternative is untenable to those who see the buffalo as wild animals because, by leaving control of buffalo, once they cross park boundaries, to the Montana Department of Livestock, it continues the killing. Besides that, wild animals are not livestock. By dealing with them as if they are, we throw away one more piece of wildness.

But because the alternative provides for the creation of special management areas outside the park where bison would be allowed and does not concentrate as broadly on brucellosis as they would have it, it is also anathema to ranchers and the Department of Livestock.

This is the most complex issue I've ever dealt with because of the whole migration of wildlife from an unfenced national park. The public lands around the park were designed as migration routes, so how do you retain any sense of wildness if you stop this?

Jeanne-Marie Souvigney, Associate Program Director for the Greater Yellowstone Coalition, working on bison issues for 10 years

The hearing was in progress when I entered the room, although no one had yet testified. People sat on folding chairs in neat rows watching an informational video on a television screen at the front of the room. An ordinary hotel meeting space, the room was one of several off a long corridor, closed off to daylight, set up with folding chairs divided by an aisle. At the back of the room a table was spread with papers and brochures presenting management plans more sympathetic to buffalo than anything written into the EIS. As you faced the front of the room, the television set for the video was on the left, the moderator at a table in the middle, and the speaker's podium on the right. The order of speakers was posted on a tripod behind the podium. Those testifying were allowed five minutes to speak. If you wanted to testify, you signed up at the table. You could do this at any time.

Looking quickly for a place to sit, I noticed an almost empty row of chairs on the side closest to the door, slid into it, sat down, then took the time to see who was there. Environmentalists and ranchers were seated on opposite sides of the aisle; ranchers on the right, environmentalists and Indians on the left. I had sat down on the ranchers' side. It was like sitting down on the wrong side at a wedding.

Men wearing cowboy boots, their cowboy hats placed beneath their chairs, were scattered throughout my side. The ranch women all sat together in the row ahead of me, as if, so long as they maintained a tight community, nothing bad could happen. All the Indians sat in the first two rows on the other side of the aisle.

In a way, I was glad I had sat where I did. I empathize with ranchers, with anyone who wants to hold on to the land instead of selling out to subdivisions. But sometimes I am frightened of their politics; frightened by their insularity; by their fear; by their dependence on the DOL. I wished I had sat behind the Indians, because that was my natural side.

So if I, believing there should be no sides, long for some kind of security, how can I fault anyone else for wanting to feel safe? My intellect and my insecurity don't match.

The first speaker introduced herself as a third-generation rancher. "We don't want to eliminate bison or anything like that. We just want management," she said, speaking nervously, apparently wishing she were somewhere else. I could identify with that. At least she had the guts to get up there and speak. "The agencies don't agree," she continued. "One agency says, let them come out of the park. One says, if you do you're going to lose your brucellosis-free status. What we want, and we want it now, is testing of all bison."

Introducing herself as a fourth-generation rancher, the next speaker spoke of the potential loss of Montana's brucellosis-free status, and therefore, the loss of her family's

way of life. Every rancher testifying introduced him- or herself as someone who had been in Montana for three or four
generations.

Then Donald Meyers, a Chippewa-Cree from the
Rocky Boy's Reservation, came to the podium. He introduced himself first in Cree, then in English. "I'm a millionth-generation Native American," he said. "We've been
here since the Creation. A lot has happened since the Corps
of Discovery came through here. We don't have too many
Native Americans left. We don't have many buffalo left
either."

*The buffalo is more than a symbol. To the Native American,
it is also a symbol, although not of the past but of the future. It is
our link to the past and, as long as the bison survive, so will we.*

Walter Fleming, a Kickapoo
from Kansas, born on the Crow Reservation, reared at
Northern Cheyenne, Associate Professor in the Depart-
ment of Native American Studies at Montana State
University, Bozeman, speaking at the Bison Boundaries
Conference held at MSU in 1992

The Indian viewpoint goes beyond the conflict between
ranchers and buffalo partisans. Indians and buffalo evolved
together on this continent. Creation stories from a number
of tribes reflect this evolution, with stories about how
human life itself is a gift of the buffalo people. The buffalo
have always been a part of plains Indian life.

"We have never forgotten the buffalo," Floyd Fisher,
buffalo manager for the Northern Cheyenne said, when he

stood to testify. "Perhaps we can work together to give the buffalo more room."

Sometimes I wonder if my longing for buffalo is not a longing for a spirituality, a connection literally embedded in the earth from whence the buffalo came. Then I have to wonder if this is what the ranchers feel—a deep connection to their land—when they perceive threats to their way of life. Are they talking about a connection with the land? If that is true, how can they not support the Indian connection to the land and all it includes? For the ranchers, is it connection to the land, or fear of losing a livelihood? Is it greed or spiritual connection?

Indians legitimize the spirituality of the thing. If it was just a bunch of white people arguing, it would never be admitted into the conversations, but when you've got them [Indians] there, it can't be ignored. I think it helps to allow the rest of us to have our spirituality too.

Author Paul Schullery, writer-editor for the Yellowstone Center for Resources

Is this what the rancher actually wants to say? Then how did it get all mixed up with brucellosis?

When we think of our environment, we don't only think of it as a physical environment, but as a spiritual environment. We have always had a spiritual relationship with the earth.

The late Bill Tallbull, chairman of the Northern Cheyenne Cultural Commission, at the Bison Boundaries Conference in 1992

Ranchers, whose living depends on maintaining their range in good enough condition that it continues to provide food for their cattle, frequently approach the buffalo question from the standpoint of range management. I think they think it allows them to be seen as concerned about the land itself. In fact, it comes off as another ploy to get rid of buffalo.

Many people think that the livestock industry wants dead bison because they want to maintain control over public lands. The last thing they want are bison established out of the park on grazing allotments. Bison, being very big animals that need a lot of grass, would definitely cut into a rancher's AUMs [the numbers of cow-calf pairs a pasture can feed per month]. The ranchers simply wouldn't be able to run as much cattle. But public land is public land. It's my land. It's your land.

D. J. Schubert, wildlife biologist representing the Fund for Animals

Our environmentalists are so conscious that we're destroying the land, the vegetation, we're doing this and that to nature and there's nothing tougher on it than that herd of buffalo. If our cattle destructed the vegetation that the buffalo do, they'd be booted out in a minute.

Keith Munns, Idaho rancher with a summer grazing allotment on Horse Butte, a few miles north of Yellowstone

Rancher Alvin Ellis is a member of the Montana Stockgrowers Association and a state legislator who ranches on the Beartooth Front west of Red Lodge, not terribly far from the northeast boundary of the park. Testifying that he had flown across Yellowstone north to Big Timber and the Shields Valley, he said he had seen willows and cottonwoods in all the drainages outside of the park, but that, in the park, the streams were "shallow and serpentine. The numbers of bison have created bad and silted streams."

Representing the Wyoming Stockgrowers Association, Lois Herbst spoke about overgrazing in Lamar Valley, the area where buffalo were ranched until the early 1950s. Lamar is a major component of the park's northern range. "Natural management is not working for the environment and its not working for the bison," she said.

It's pretty well concluded that the grassland on the northern range is certainly not overgrazed.

Wayne Brewster, deputy director of the Yellowstone Center for Resources

One blizzarding afternoon the preceding winter, Wayne Brewster and I sat in my living room talking about the park's grassland. He told me that extensive studies done on the northern range show it as healthy. Unfortunately, the DOL and the ranchers don't trust the park, or its information, any more than they do the environmentalists, the animal rightists, or the Indians.

Carolyn Duckworth lives at the edge of the park. She spends a good deal of time in it, both privately and teaching classes at the Yellowstone Institute. After listening to people testifying about an overgrazed park, she presented her own testimony. "Folks, the parts of the park that look overgrazed are semidesert. In the interior, in the lush grasslands, you can't even see a grizzly."

I thought about a grizzly bear I couldn't see in tall grass. Working with Yellowstone horsepacking outfitter Richard Clark, I spend most of the summer in the park backcountry on horseback, pulling a string of mules. One windless afternoon a few weeks before the hearing, as we rode through the Pelican Valley, I noticed the grass moving along the right side of the trail a few yards ahead. I stopped my horse and mules. The grizzly jumped out of the grass, ran across the trail in front of us, and disappeared into the woods.

Jennie Parker, a Northern Cheyenne, is a member of her Tribal Council Executive Committee. "It's not the buffalo's problem," she said. "It's the people's problem." A rancher, Jennie Parker also works with the tribal buffalo. For her, the two are not mutually exclusive. "The buffalo is a sacred symbol within our ceremonies," she said. "We revere the buffalo in a sacred manner. Our state of Montana and other states, Congress, pass numerous laws for the protection of these beautiful animals," she said, "then they break their own laws. We need to address this problem."

Listen to the wind, listen to the trees. Walk out on the prairies by yourself. Find the environment that is there. It has never changed. The spiritual environment has never changed.
Bill Tallbull

Jennie Parker's name was the last on the sign-up list posted at the front of the room. "As a Cheyenne, the woman is always the last to talk. As the last speaker, I'm going to take two more minutes," she said as the moderator held up the one-minute sign. "I'm sorry, but that's not possible," the moderator interrupted, following the rules.

Without a glance at the moderator, the Cheyenne woman simply stopped speaking, walked away from the podium, gathered her things at the back of the room, and left the hearing. The hearing was scheduled to continue into the evening regardless of whether anybody else turned up.

Other people began drifting in, but after Jennie Parker left, things seemed finished to me. It seemed time to go, as if everything had been said. I handed my testimony to a person collecting written testimony and walked out into the still-hot afternoon.

I had all the words spoken at this hearing in my notebook and on my tape recorder. Back in Bozeman, I compared them with all the other words I have in notebooks and on tape. It took weeks to do this. I could not make them into music. A collage, maybe. One made of muddy, brilliant, pale, bold, muted, deep colors. A collage or an odd kind of rainbow. One that skips the pot of gold to end in a buffalo wallow on one side, the manure-thick mud of a rancher's holding pen on the other. Either way, it's more or less brown. When I was in college somebody put a notice on the bulletin board in the student union that said, LIFE IS A BUCKET OF SHIT WITH THE HANDLES ON THE INSIDE. Perhaps this is an apt summation of the politics of buffalo.

On the other hand, it does not account for history. Paul Schullery, who is a historian, looks at the long haul.

Talking about the winter of 1996–97, when over 1,100 buffalo were killed, he said, "Everybody is panicky that this herd may be down to two thousand, when we were down to thirty or forty once. That doesn't make me feel too much better about the two thousand, but it helps me understand that they are, after all, bison and they're very good at making new bison."

Paul brings a measure of reason, of poetry, and of hope to the park's struggles to come to grips with the dilemmas—including the buffalo problem—in which it consistently finds itself. In Paul's way of seeing, nothing is isolated. Everything has its place in the scheme of things. Everything, us included, is connected. This puts buffalo in a different context. It puts ranchers in a different context, too. It even, for God's sake, puts the DOL in a different context.

But is anybody listening?

HOME ON THE RANGE

Oh give me a home
Where the buffalo roam
Where the deer and the antelope play
Where seldom is heard a discouraging word
And the skies are not cloudy all day

IT'S the song I grew up on, a theme, a longing for open space and a wild place, a lullaby, all given to me at birth in my father's singing. I didn't know what the place was, or where, or what it meant, but I knew it existed. My father hadn't been in that place either, except once to pass through it on a troop train to Oklahoma and Texas. I guess he saw something of Texas. *His* father used to go out west to buy horses to sell back east. My father must have gotten it from the stories his father told. By the time the stories got to me, the place was mythic.

When my father finally moved to Montana he was 92 years old, often out of the mind the rest of us had always known, and four months away from death. The myth no longer mattered to him. Once, on a drive from Bozeman to Harrison, looking out the truck window at miles and miles of open, rolling ranchland, he said, "There's an awful lot of space here."

The only buffalo he ever saw was as a small boy in Oswego, New York, when he sat in the audience at Buffalo Bill's Wild West Show. "What was it like?" I asked him, meaning the show. "He was a handsome man," my father said, meaning Buffalo Bill.

It is hard for me to justify the glamour of a man who earned his name (in 1867) by killing buffalo (on contract, 12 a day) for the railroad. But at least the guy was a good shot.

In summer 1997 Yellowstone Park and the Buffalo Bill Historical Center in Cody, Wyoming, collaborated on a buffalo exhibit at Yellowstone's Canyon Visitor Center. Entitled "Where the Buffalo Roam," the collection of photos, artwork, quotes, statements, dioramas, and interactive displays—scheduled well before the preceding, devastating winter—was organized around the lyrics to "Home on the Range." It is a song that seems not so much to have been written as to have sprung out of the West, like a sagebrush or an antelope, something that was always there, something any of us can claim as our own. It is my father's lullaby, a song that is my birthright.

The track of a single buffalo leads from the exhibit's entrance into its core—a display of the buffalo's history since the arrival of the white man; its habits and habitat; its role in nature's scheme of things; its place as symbol—of plenty, of wildness, of balance, of controversy, of the machinations of the human mind.

Many of the photos focus on the death of buffalo. The nineteenth-century version. Among them is one made in 1880 of a 50-foot-high mountain of buffalo skulls. A man stands at the base of the mountain with his foot on a skull. Another man stands at the top, in the same pose. Although the men are dwarfed by the mountain of skulls, they seem mindless of how small they are. Indeed, their stance is proprietary, as if they were masters of this domain. What is it to be master of a domain of dead buffalo . . . ?

Other photos show buffalo being shot from a Kansas Pacific Railroad car. The Kansas Pacific is the railroad that hired Buffalo Bill, but, of course, he shot from the back of a running horse. How easily the buffalo were shot from the train. There is not much drama to shooting buffalo, or daring, or skill, unless one does it as Buffalo Bill, or as Indians did; mounted, or luring them over a jump. It is possible to both admire the Indian kill and hate Buffalo Bill's kill, and still respect the skill and the daring of each. There is nothing to admire in the photo of a prairie littered with the bodies of buffalo shot from a train.

When the killing rose into the thousands, little was taken from the dead buffalo on the prairie. Left to rot, perhaps they have entered some sacred mountain we cannot even see. According to an old Kiowa story, the buffalo, which were once everywhere, loved the people and provided them with everything they needed for life: food, shelter, utensils; so many things. The animal was a regular general store. But then the whites came and built the railroad, cutting the people's lands in half. The buffalo fought for the people, tearing up the tracks and chasing away the whites' cattle. So the army was sent to kill the buffalo. The army brought in hunters, who killed until the bones of the buffalo covered the land and the buffalo saw they could no longer fight.

One morning a Kiowa woman who had gone to get water saw something moving in the mist. As the mist parted, an old buffalo cow came out of it, one of the old buffalo women that led the herds. Behind her were the last few young buffalo warriors plus a few calves and young cows. The old buffalo cow led the herd straight toward the side of a mountain that opened as they approached. They entered the mountain. The Kiowa woman caught a glimpse inside where the earth was green and new, the sun shone, and meadowlarks sang. It looked as the world had looked before the whites came. Then the mountain closed behind them and the buffalo were gone.

In their death, it is their life that haunts us. A pen and ink drawing called *The Herd, 1860* shows a line of buffalo fronting a river of buffalo stretching solid across an entire valley, as if the valley had been flooded with them. The drawing was made in 1913, by which time there had been no buffalo on the plains for over twenty-five years.

The buffalo's track leads past a diorama in which a huge buffalo lies on his back, his legs thrust up at the top point of his roll in a wallow. His coat is full and thick and covered with the soft dust of the wallow. I was sure that if I watched long enough, I would see the buffalo move. It seemed only a matter of time before he stood. He would roll back and up and stand like a statue, rooted to the earth and to time and to his own being. I have seen it so often in Yellowstone. What I am seeing is 10,000 years of time. Our interruption, deadly as it has been, is so short.

A small child near me stared at the buffalo, then turned to his mother. "Mama, is it dead?" he asked.

"No, honey, it's just sleeping."

Patches of a buffalo's summer and winter coats are displayed for visitors to touch. They provide as unequivocal an understanding of the difference between seasons here as any meteorologist could present. The summer coat is thin and stringy, the winter coat so thick my hand hardly gets to the bottom of it. The coat itself is like the coat of the dead buffalo whose head I touched last winter. I could not get my hand through his coat either, but the difference is that his coat was connected to an animal alive a few minutes earlier. There was nothing abstract about his coat.

The words to "Home on the Range" are displayed along the top of the walls, hovering there like some message from heaven. Beneath "where the buffalo roam and the deer and the antelope play," is a blow-up of a map of the Greater Yellowstone Ecosystem. "Ecosystems do not follow human boundaries," the accompanying statement reads. "Although

Yellowstone National Park's borders have been set by humans, nature does not recognize these limits.

"The Park's buffalo are part of the Greater Yellowstone Ecosystem, an area which includes not only the Park, but also the surrounding region—an area of approximately 18 million acres . . . What happens to one organism in the ecosystem affects the others, and buffalo are an important part of the web of relationships."

I can't figure out how ecosystems ever end. When you come to the edges of a particular defined ecosystem, are they not intertwined with the edges of the next? Latitudes and longitudes and climate and terrain change, of course, but it seems to me there is only one ecosystem on the earth, and even that must be intertwined at its heavenly limits with the stars.

In updating the exhibit to reflect the preceding winter's difficulties, the organizers have—under "a discouraging word"—added a quote from Montana Governor Marc Racicot, reported in the April 7, 1997, *Billings Gazette*. "The unfettered roaming of infected animals is just not something that will be allowed by other states or the federal government."

What he is saying is that Montana has no choice; that other states will not allow Montana cattle across their borders and the federal government's Animal and Plant Health Inspection Service won't allow it either. But it comes across wrong. It spreads the idea that all Yellowstone buffalo are diseased and that those people fighting for a fair deal for buffalo are talking about something beyond letting them roam on public land adjacent to the park. It seems inflammatory to me. Unnecessary. One more thing to harden the positions.

In this section of the exhibit, a National Park Service photo shows buffalo being shot by Montana Department of Livestock personnel in winter of 1997. One animal has been stopped, half fallen forever; another stands forever in the shooter's sights.

"Because of the controversy surrounding buffalo leaving the Park," a statement on the wall reads, "the future of Yellowstone's free-ranging buffalo herd remains in doubt. There are few places left in the world where humans and wild animals co-exist without conflict. Do wild animals have a place in the modern world? What will it mean if we lose our remaining natural heritage? What will be the long-term consequences to humans if wild animals disappear?"

No one has stopped in front of this statement.

There is, though, a large crowd backed up in front of a video of a couple of tourists standing too close to a buffalo. The narrator points out that the buffalo raises his tail to indicate this. A man, who doesn't get the signal, is simply tossed aside by the buffalo. He looks like a plaything, lightly tossed up in the air, as if he had no weight, no bones. People stand in front of this, fascinated.

Of Yellowstone's three million annual tourists, fewer than 21,000 go even a mile into the backcountry. But even from the roads they have seen animals and thermal features and forests and burned forests, glorious meadows, sparkling rivers, and a sky where eagles fly. They will actually have seen more animals than most of us in the backcountry

where animals are shyer, wilder, less used to human presence; where they do not cluster in such herds; where the
sight of a single old bull buffalo becomes a moment of wonder; where the cry of a redtail pierces the territory of
silence; where the crashing of a moose through the brush or
a bear walking out of forest into sun tears into some primal
place we share.

The tourists on the roads may experience less of the
country but they will have marveled at the animals. Many of
them will have stopped dead in the middle of a roadway to
marvel, causing yet another of those frequent Yellowstone
buffalo or bear or elk jams. Still, even under these circum-
stances, they will experience some form of wildness, for
wildness makes its own accommodations. If tourists connect
to wildness in its form as roadside attraction, it is a beginning. They may not take in the whole—animal and land and
hour and season and sun and wind—but what they do experience may encourage them to go deeper. Certainly, it
encouraged some to visit the buffalo exhibit. Regardless of
the traffic passing by, and the crowds around them, some
will have experienced awe.

On a large bulletin board near the exhibit's exit there is a
sign urging visitors to PLEASE SHARE WITH US YOUR FEELINGS
ABOUT PRESERVING THE BUFFALO. A writing board, pens, and
paper are provided. The messages are periodically cleared
from the bulletin board to make room for more. Some notes
are in the handwriting of children, others clearly adult.

"Please, please let us take care of the buffalo. Don't kill
them! Preserve them!!! Thank you."

"We should keep them because they are really cool."

"Neat animals."

"SAVE THEM."

"If one person tries to save or help them, maybe it will influence others!!! *I'll try.*"

"Stop killing the buffalo! Can't we learn from our past mistakes?"

"Please control the human herds—not an extinct animal herd—they cannot be replaced."

"Do Not shoot the buffalo!!!!" [with a buffalo head drawing].

"Buffulos *[sic]* Rule"

"Save the bison at all costs. Sacrifice cattle if necessary, but not the bison."

"Without bison it wouldn't be the same."

"If you kill one more buffalo I kill you." [The writer of this noted he was from Buffalo, New York.]

"Control migration out of park. Encourage migration to lower elevations within park."

"Gov. Racicot! Shame on you."

"Don't groom the roads in winter and it will be harder for the buffalo to leave."

"Let the buffalo do what they have been doing for many years, Montana."

On a small wall leading out of the exhibit, there is a reproduction of a poster from Buffalo Bill's Wild West Show of 1900. The poster shows Colonel W. F. Cody's face in a circle superimposed on the side of a running buffalo.

Jesus

he was a handsome man

e. e. cummings wrote of Buffalo Bill in *Portraits* in the 1920s. The same words my father used sixty years later. My father did not read e. e. cummings.

Underneath the handsome face and the running buffalo, written in big letters, are the words—I AM COMING.

Which of you, I wondered.

BUFFALO SKULL

AS part of our tour of the Rocky Boy's Reservation, Don Meyers took me to see a sweat lodge. Outside the lodge, as is traditional, there is a large fire pit to heat the stones used for the sweat. Directly across from the fire pit is the door to a modest house. We entered the house. The sweat lodge, built of bent willows in the traditional way, then covered with blankets and quilts, is set up inside the living room space.

"Isn't that odd?" I asked Don.

"It's an accommodation," he said.

Like using the steer's head until they got a buffalo skull in the Sun Dance, I thought. These people are used to making accommodations.

A length of carpet extends the few feet from the lodge entrance to an altar set up opposite the entrance.

"There is supposed to be a buffalo skull on the altar," Don said.

The altar is bare. Here, too, Don has shown me the buffalo's absence.

BUFFALO HEART

I DROVE the Hi-Line from Chinook to the Fort Belknap Reservation straight into the rising sun. A giant red ball hanging just above the northern plains, the sun filled the horizon. Blinding when you looked directly at it; it was impossible to look anywhere else. I fought to keep my eyes down, on the centerline of the road, but they were inexorably pulled back, as if the sun were my destination.

The Hi-Line is country of space and wind. Wheat country. Buffalo country. Sudden ranges of mountains insert themselves as if to insist there are other ways of life, but they are always at some blue distance; always like some sacred dream.

Someone in Chinook told me I could get breakfast at Dee's Diner in Harlem, four miles this side of Fort Belknap. When a sign pointed left to Harlem, I turned toward town. Seeing a row of old pickups parked on Main Street, I assumed a café; the place where the local men meet for coffee before work every morning of their lives. There was no café. There was nothing on Main Street but closed shops and the old pickups. Maybe this is pickup heaven, where the old ones go when they die. Returning to the Hi-Line highway, Route 2, I found Dee's Diner farther down the road, conveniently located so you can just slip past the town without knowing it is there.

Fort Belknap, home to Gros Ventre and Assiniboine, was created for the Gros Ventre in 1889. The Assiniboine, along with the Sioux, had been assigned land on the much larger Fort Peck Reservation farther east, but a number of them drifted west to Fort Belknap and stayed. A Sioux people, the Assiniboine separated from the Yanktoni Sioux in the early 1600s, after the wives of two tribal leaders quarreled over a delicacy—a buffalo heart.

I had arranged to meet Mike Fox at 9:30. As director of the reservation's Fish & Game Department, Mike is responsible for the reservation buffalo. He is, in fact, responsible for an extraordinary success story. Since coming to Fish & Game in 1990 (hired because four years in the Coast Guard had provided him with the requisite law enforcement background), he has grown a herd of 50 or 60 animals pastured on 2,000 acres into a herd of over 400 on 22,000 acres.

Looking for his office, I circled the tribal complex buildings, just off Route 2, several times before someone directed me to a huge, metal, hangarlike building that also serves as a kind of warehouse and bingo hall. The department's offices occupy a small niche in the building. They are like an after-thought, a temporary camp. It is as far from Route 2 as you can get and still be in the agency area; well beyond the Community College, the BIA and tribal offices, the new hospital, the old hospital, tracts of government houses.

I checked in with the secretary, early for our appointment. She told me Mike had called to say he would be late. I waited in an antechamber furnished with five plastic chairs and decorated with pen and ink drawings of two Gros Ventre leaders and two Assiniboine warriors mounted on colored construction paper and hung on the wall. I heard the cry of a hawk. It was insistent, as if it was trapped in the building. I asked the secretary if there was a bird somewhere in the office. Her computer, she said.

A fluffy white toy buffalo sat on the shelf next to the coffeemaker in her office; a pint milk container on one of the plastic chairs. There were no windows; just the hawk's cry of the computer and the drone of some kind of machine, perhaps a heating unit. The warehouse beyond the offices was filled with a hollow, damp cold.

When Mike arrived, we stopped briefly in his office before heading out to see the tribal buffalo. A stack of buffalo robes lay on the floor next to his desk, for use on vision quests. (Seeking visions through isolation, exposure to the elements, and fasting is a plains Indian ritual. Practiced in the hope of receiving a sign from a supernatural being that can appear in the guise of a bird, an animal, a plant, a stone, an ancestor, or virtually anything else, it is a way—if one has prepared properly—of receiving a power, a *medicine*. The thing seen in the vision becomes the person's guardian spirit.) I wondered how many Fish & Game offices around the country aid in vision quests.

In the big, shiny Fish & Game truck, we headed down a long, straight road through autumn-brown pastures; Route 66, which crosses the reservation from north to south—50 miles of lonesome highway.

The first buffalo arrived at Fort Belknap in 1974. About 27 head, half from the National Bison Range in Moise, half from Theodore Roosevelt National Park in South Dakota, were kept at tribal headquarters for use at powwows, Sun Dances, and other ceremonies. Four years later they were moved out to Snake Butte, a landmark in the west-central part of the reservation—to which we were headed—where the tribes had a little over 2,000 fenced-in acres. The number of animals was kept low, the excess distributed to the various communities scattered across the reservation. Then Mike took over at Fish & Game, began meeting with other tribes, and discovered the Crow tribe had over 1,000 animals. "I thought, wow, *we* should be that," he told me. "That's what *we* should be doing!"

Until Mike's tenure, care of the buffalo cost the tribal government money and the animals were regarded as a burden. When they overgrazed their allotted 2,000 acres—not hard to do in a dry land—it was necessary to purchase hay to feed them throughout the year. If they broke out of their allotted space—a natural thing for a buffalo to do when looking for food—the tribal government had to hire somebody to chase them back in.

Mike arrived on the scene with a different vision. He believed the herd could be self-sustaining, if its size was increased and it was given more country to graze. He proved his point the first fall they sold enough calves to meet the department's operating budget, freeing it from relying on the tribal government for the year's funding. "When we got that jack," Mike said, "it was a pretty good victory for me!"

While it might seem odd that a people for whom the buffalo had once been literally of life importance would not automatically be behind a buffalo program on the reservation, too many tribal members—the elders and the parents and grandparents of the elders—were forced, spiritually and culturally, into separation from the buffalo. According to Mike, about a third of the people now living on the reservation retain their culture and language; another third hold some links to it, and the last third are completely removed. "Especially the ranching families," Mike said. Although he comes from a ranching family, his upbringing included traditional Gros Ventre ways. "It seems like the ranching community are the ones that have the biggest mistrust of the buffalo; that they're going to take over," Mike said. The Chairman (elected head of the tribal government or council) in office the first year the buffalo earned money was a rancher. The current chairman is a rancher. Most people on the Council come from a ranching background.

Snake Butte lay ahead of us, its granite walls rising a thousand feet above the prairie's miles of flat land. Mike turned the truck off Route 66 onto a dirt road, stopping before a closed gate at the bottom of the butte. "You see what keeps our buffalo in," he said, motioning toward a four-strand barbed-wire fence that seemed to encircle the butte.

The fence didn't look like much to me. I doubted it would look like much to a buffalo. "Why do they stay in here and the ranchers up around Yellowstone say that they can't fence them out?" I asked.

"If you provide them with food and water, they'll stay," Mike said.

"Do you feed them?" I asked.

"No. We'll probably buy 10 tons of hay just in case we get into a bad situation in the spring where it doesn't rain and the grass isn't growing. That's only for emergency purposes. We ran into that about four years ago . . . a real dry spring and just nothing grew. Then we only had 4,000 acres. Now we got 10,000." (When we met at Fort Belknap, the new range that would bring the acreage up to 22,000 was not yet in use.)

Two days before I arrived, someone had left the gate in front of us open. About 250 buffalo walked out. Mike had seen them about two miles north earlier in the day but, at that distance and in that place, assumed they were cattle. It was not until evening that he noticed the open gate and, looking through binoculars, discovered the cattle were buffalo. Because getting them back from that distance was a two- or three-hour job that could not be finished before dark, Mike decided to leave it until the next day. By then, however, the council had been informed the buffalo were out. They wanted immediate action. "The council was screaming, 'Get 'em in!' " Mike said. He told them he would do it in the morning.

In the morning, Mike could not find the buffalo. They no longer grazed where they were last seen. Wondering what to do as he and his wardens drove toward the gate, Mike rounded the last curve in the road to see the buffalo, standing about a hundred yards from the gate.

"Within ten minutes we had 'em in," Mike said. "They had themselves in, I should say. But that's the same thing with Yellowstone. They're gonna go where the food and water are. And when you've got real heavy snowfall, and it's hard to get feed, they're gonna go to where it's easier to find feed. That's the survival instinct they have.

"We had a problem here when we had that real dry spring. They were constantly breaking through the fence. They wouldn't *break* through. They would *walk* through. Because they were gonna go where there was food.

"But these guys are so acclimated to this area—I've had other animals get out and it's almost the same thing. Where a rancher would go racing after 'em and herd 'em back in, lot of times, you just wait."

Beyond the gate, the road circles the butte to come out on top of it. Mike parked the truck on the dry brown grass. The ground was strewn with granite boulders and broken by rocky outcroppings. A steep, long drop below us, the prairie stretched for miles, interrupted to the west by the distant forms of the Bear's Paw Mountains, to the south by the Little Rockies. All around us, the land flowed like oceans to the sky. Because the tribes have always had an aversion to cutting into Mother Earth in order to farm, the prairie extending across most of the reservation is one of the most intact native shortgrass prairies in Montana. The blue gramma and crested wheat grass—buffalo grass—is the grass that was always here.

"Buffalo make better use of this grass than a beef cow does," Mike said. "They get more out of what they eat than a cow does because they've adapted to it for so long."

This country is probably as close to being what it was 200 years ago as it is currently possible to get. The only thing not intact is the Little Rockies, the range bordering the reservation on the south. In 1895, when white men discovered gold in them, the tribes were more or less boondoggled out of mountains they considered sacred and that were part of the original reservation lands. The mountains have since been literally torn apart; the streams issuing from them onto the reservation polluted by cyanide used in the mining process. I did not ask Mike about this. I was here to talk about buffalo.

"There are some old bulls that usually hang out around here," Mike said, looking for them. I had noticed several as we drove up, but they disappeared into a slight dip when we parked.

The land looked dry, in spite of a large pond in our view. But there are springs around the butte, and the tribes have built several stock ponds. Two intermittent streams in the area hold water much of the year.

With considerable pride, Mike pointed out the pasture boundaries, saying that, when he first got out there, he thought the original 2,000 acres was good. But when he started thinking about increasing the acreage in order to increase the number of buffalo, he went to the council and asked for the butte. "I said, 'Cows don't make use of it anyway,'" he told me.

"They said, 'Yeah, but you take just the butte. You can't take any of the flat land.'

"So you can see where the fence goes. It just tucks right around the butte. But then I asked for this area over here," he said, pointing off to the right. "I told them, 'Look, it's just a dry lake and there's nothing but gumbo and hardpan out there. It's not going to take that much out of grazing for the cows.' They said, 'Okay, take a little bit more, and that's it.'"

Two years later, Mike discovered that an Indian rancher was subleasing to a non-Indian rancher. He went back to the council, offering to pay a higher rate for that land if they turned it over to the buffalo program.

"I expected all these questions about the expected growth of the herd and potential income, lease income, all this, you know," Mike said. "Before I could even get into my spiel, somebody made a motion that the request be approved and they voted and I walked out of there and went, 'Wait now . . . something's wrong here.'" We both laughed.

"The worst-case scenario," he continued, "is that you're going to end up with a thousand animals that are at least the same value as domestic cows. At least! This beats any other thing that you can think of doing, like building a factory out here that'll be a white elephant in a couple of years. If all else fails, at least you've got something to eat."

"So are you aiming to outdo the Crow?" I asked.

Mike laughed. "Not so much to outdo 'em," he said. "Our main goal is to bring the buffalo back into the daily lives of the tribal people."

For Mike, this means the buffalo should be available to everyone on the reservation as part of a healthy diet and as an essential part of ceremonies—such as the Sun Dance that requires a skull—or of vision quests or fasts where there should be a buffalo robe to sit on.

The idea of buffalo as a normal part of the people's diet again is vital to Mike. Accustomed to buffalo meat for thousands of years, Indian people have suffered serious health problems since its loss. Extremely high instances of high blood pressure, cholesterol problems, heart conditions, and diabetes on the reservations can be traced to it. "All of a sudden the diet switched from almost a perfect diet—low cholesterol, low fat—to a government diet," Mike said. "You know, bringing in the pork fat and, later on, canned meat with the high-fat, high-salt content. Any other community, you will not have the kind of diabetes you have among the tribes. If we can get back to that diet we evolved with along with the buffalo, it won't cure all of the problems, but it will sure as heck help."

Buffalo meat is the meat of choice—for traditional as well as health reasons—for any sort of event or celebration on the reservation. Fish & Game keeps it on hand to do away with requests for a whole buffalo for a small event where 20 pounds of stew meat would suffice. If a family, having a hard time, requests a deer tag in order to go out and shoot some meat, the department will give them 50 pounds of buffalo meat instead. (More meat, Mike points out, than most deer produce after being dressed.)

The department works closely with reservation social services to provide buffalo meat free of charge to people in need of help but ineligible for welfare or food stamps for a certain time.

"And we kind of reward ourselves every now and then," Mike said, looking pleased at the thought. "The program employees, if we field-dress them ourselves, we'll take home a roast or something. It's a labor-intensive process. It makes me more appreciative of my ancestors, what they had to go through. When you're skinning these animals out, your knife, with the hair, gets dull so fast, it's unbelievable."

Buffalo taken for ceremonies are killed in a sacred manner, although always under the direct supervision of Fish & Game. The ceremonial committee is presented a choice of three or four animals. Whether shot by a member of that committee or by Fish & Game, the killing is preceded and accompanied by the appropriate prayers. "The Sun Dance society sometimes takes two hours before they can shoot a buffalo," Mike said, laughing.

"Do I detect a little impatience there?" I asked.

Until Mike took over at Fish & Game, people, given a buffalo by the council for a particular occasion, simply went out to the pasture and took what they wanted—often the biggest bull they could find, or a young cow or heifer because they thought the meat would be tenderer. As a result, there were no old bulls in the herd, and the herd's ability to produce calves was limited.

By instituting a policy of taking only young bulls, leaving some to age, Mike has built up a herd with a normal social order *and* the ability to increase relatively fast.

"The young bulls," Mike said, "they're like the warrior class of the buffalo. They'll give their lives so the people can eat. The old cows, they're like grandmothers to me. The calves you see out here will be producing *their* calves when I'm retired. Some environmentalists want to let them all roam until they die of old age. No, that's not what the Creator put them here for."

To cut down on inbreeding, animals are brought in from outside the reservation. In recent years 3 bulls arrived from Moise, four young bulls were traded with the Sioux for four young bulls, and 20 head came from Wind Cave National Park. Mike feels that's enough. "We've reached a point where we can actually expand the herd as fast as we want," he said.

We stood looking out over the vast expanse of prairie spreading below Snake Butte. Mike said he had something to show me. "We can drive down to this rock right around the corner here," he said, turning back to the truck. "We can walk, but the snakes might be out yet." The truck wobbled and twisted over large boulders and rough terrain on the edge of the drop-off.

"Are you sure you wouldn't rather walk?" I asked, thinking snakes are nothing compared to a truck driven by a Montana man, a race born believing trucks are horses with wheels.

"We could . . . I just don't like snakes, though," he said.

We climbed out of the truck below a tumble of boulders. Mike told me that, earlier, he had come here to place a buffalo skull on the rocks to bleach. "I was walking along and I saw this thing," he said, looking down. At our feet was a large, flat black rock with a buffalo carved into it. The buffalo stood with its head down, as if grazing. At first I mistook its horns for legs. The same thing had happened to Mike, when he came upon it. "I thought it was missing a head," he said. "I had chills when I found it. Especially when I thought it was a headless one and I was putting skulls up here."

The outline was perfect when Mike found it. Archaeologists have told him it is at least 200 years old. He has pictures of how it looked. But now a part of it has been chipped away. "A lot of people didn't know it was here until I seen it," Mike said, sadly, I thought. "I almost think I should fence it off at times," he said. "At least, it would give people the idea that, yes, we know it's here. Put a sign here, PLEASE DO NOT DAMAGE THIS."

"It's a shame to fence it off," I said.

"Exactly. You're ruining the whole area.

"Those rocks up there," he continued, "this obviously had to be used for some type of buffalo jump because of the gradual slope from the east and the drop-off in some areas. This being here, then returning the buffalo back here; especially even allowing them to be back on the butte, it's full circle. They were meant to be here.

"They must have spent a lot of time up there, because, just like this, there's carving of buffalo hoofprints up there. When I'm sure the snakes are gone, I'll look again."

"Like about January," I suggested.

We drove across vast pastures toward a large herd of buffalo we had been seeing in the distance. One huge group grazed off to the left, another almost straight ahead, spread across the dirt track we drove. "They've been split up in two separate herds as the numbers have grown. This is about the closest I've seen them together," Mike said.

Although there are a few fences stretching across the pastures, the buffalo are not separated by fences. All inner gates are left open so the animals have full run of the place.

Mike had tried rotational grazing, deciding, in accord with his livestock background, to let an area rest that had been used for ten years. "So I shut 'em out," he said. "Locked all the gates. Come back the next day and the herd was right back in here. You'll see these animals in every corner of these ten thousand acres throughout the week. Whereas, hot days, cattle will almost never leave the reservoirs."

There are about 300 adult buffalo on the reservation and a little over 100 calves. Forty percent of the calves are sold; 60 percent are retained for the tribal herd. Last year the buffalo program took in approximately $88,000, returning $30,000 to the tribal government. "We only needed $60,000 to operate," Mike said. "We said it was for the lease of the land. This year they said, 'No, we don't want you to do that because some people are saying that you're just giving us this money. When, in fact, you should pay for the land.' I said, 'That's fine, because the land is only $21,000 per year in the lease.'"

"So, in other words, you're making money here," I said.

Mike laughed. "Yeah."

We passed old tipi rings as we drove. "They're all over," Mike said. "This whole area must have been used quite a bit, probably because of that spring back there." Before the 1700s, Blackfeet and Cree were here. The Gros Ventres, closely allied with the Blackfeet, arrived in the early 1700s. Mike is Gros Ventre. His wife is Assiniboine.

Mike stopped the truck to look at the buffalo herd ahead of us, excited by what he saw. "If they're all spread out on that flat up there, it's something I've just gotta stop and look at," he said.

It is, indeed, awesome—buffalo spread out across the prairie, as natural as the grass and sky in the hugeness of this landscape; natural and miraculous. How extraordinary it must be for Mike who, after all, has done this.

"How did you feel about buffalo before you started working with them?" I asked.

"Almost ambivalent," he said. "It was really neither here nor there, because the herd was so small. It's like that commercial selling buffalo wings, that chicken deal, and the kid says, 'Aren't those extinct?' That's a lot of people's thought—they're extinct. I thought, growing up, oh, there's a few in zoos and a few in parks, but they'll never come back. Never be a part of the tribe's way of life again. I think a lot of people think it's so far from being a reality that they just push it off. Until you start working with them, until you start being associated with them, you don't realize the possibilities of what can happen."

We drove on, directly into the herd. A buffalo with a yellow ear tag watched us approach. "See that old cow looking at us now?" Mike asked. "That is an original cow from 1974."

Few of the buffalo are tagged. Most that are, are run for the InterTribal Bison Cooperative. The tags remind Mike that those animals belong to ITBC and not to the reservation.

The InterTribal Bison Cooperative, headquartered in Rapid City, South Dakota, was formed in 1992 to provide assistance in restoring buffalo to tribal lands. They provide on-the-ground help to the tribes in setting up bison management plans. They are also a source of bison, receiving about 25 percent (or more) of the surplus bison from various refuges. The tribes submit their proposals for that surplus and, based on their ability to take care of them, ITBC determines how many go where. The only costs to the tribes are their percentage of ITBC's roundup costs and expenses, and transportation to the reservation.

Several buffalo eyed the truck, but most continued grazing as if we were not there. A few late calves, still red, stared at the truck from the safety of their mothers' sides. Four antelope stood at the far edge of the herd.

We climbed out of the truck into the warm October morning. The scent of sage surrounded us. Buffalo grazed sand-colored grass covering a sand-colored earth. Some, watching us, flared their nostrils. A bull lowered himself into a wallow, making a snuffling sound as he sank into it to roll. The breathing of several hundred buffalo was like a drum tattoo; their deep grunts a cello counterpoint.

What must it have been to see them by the thousands . . . to hear them by the thousands . . .

"There's Crooked Horn," Mike said, pointing out a buffalo with a smashed horn. Earlier we had passed Evil Eye, who has an errant tuft of hair over his forehead that makes him look mean. According to Mike, his looks and his personality mesh. A big, heavy, eight-year-old bull, he seems to have been through some wars. When I asked Mike if he would choose a bull like Evil Eye to shoot when a buffalo was requested, he said it was important to keep the renegade genes, the wild genes, in the herd.

Although most animals are not named (some, like Evil Eye and Crooked Horn, just *naturally* got names), Mike knows many of them as individuals. He *sees* the differences in individual animals as well as differences between buffalo from Moise and those from Teddy Roosevelt. When he pointed out shorter heads held lower and stubbier horns on the Moise bulls than on the Roosevelt bulls, I began identifying every animal I saw. One becomes an expert so quickly.

Moving like the tide, the buffalo ebbed away from us. A bald eagle soared above them, above us, silent in his flight.

Driving away from the herd, across a dried gumbo earth, we arrived at a prairie dog colony. There was a big colony beyond the buffalo herd, too, but it was too far away for me to make out much besides the tan, dried mud.

To find buffalo and prairie dogs together is natural. Buffalo wallow in the colonies, of which there are many on the reservation. In a good season, Mike told me, the growth is better in prairie dog colonies because the grass is constantly eaten down to grow back. It is always new. But I see no new grass now, in late October. This is the edge of winter in northern Montana, however hot the sun.

The huge numbers of prairie dogs also makes this a natural place for black-footed ferrets, which eat them. Ferrets have recently been reintroduced. Last year, 23 were freed on the reservation. In the spring, three were found—two males and one female, but she got lost during the breeding season. Only one of the males is still around. Fifty-two more were released this year. So far, only 10 of those have been located.

"We're just going to have to keep dumping ferrets and dumping ferrets until we get some wild-born kits," Mike said. "Until we start getting some production out of the wild-born kits, it's gonna be a fairly long process."

A biologist from the Montana Department of Fish, Wildlife & Parks drove up to check on a site where a ferret was seen the previous night. He said a coyote had been sitting out on the bluff behind us, watching the whole operation. I guess a lot of creatures here are interested in what is going on. At the entrances to their burrows, dozens and dozens of prairie dogs stood watching, sometimes in pairs, the colony filled with the sound of their chirping. All these animals—the prairie dogs and the coyotes, the antelope and the eagles and the buffalo—must find the behavior of humans so odd. So little that we do results in eating anything.

"The prairie dogs are huge," I said.

"Maybe that's why we're losing so many ferrets," the biologist said.

It was a long drive back across the brown grass and gumbo earth to the buffalo corrals. As we drove up, two big old bulls loitering around the corrals stared at the truck. I wondered if they might charge, but one just watched and the other moved slightly off to the side of the truck track, lay down in a wallow, and rolled, letting us know who's territory we were entering. We drove far enough past him to pose no challenge before getting out of the truck. Mike and I agreed with him. It is his territory.

The corrals consist of an elaborate system of alleys and gates and pens, all of them boarded up—like those in Yellowstone and on the Gunderson ranch—so the buffalo inside cannot see daylight and, in an attempt to reach it, become more agitated than they already are. There are high ramps around the corral sides so the men can work the buffalo from above. They work speedily, getting the first animals out—the ones they do not want to keep—within an hour.

"We try not to get the bulls in," Mike said. "Usually they're separated from the herd then, anyway. So we'll make an effort to chase the bulls out of sight."

The roundup is done in late fall when cold weather makes the buffalo easier to handle.

"Their metabolism kind of slows down a little bit," Mike said. "They aren't so spooky. Like right now, I can drive right in the middle of the herd with my truck, they'll hardly notice me. But get one or two more vehicles, sometimes even a strange vehicle, they'll take off. It's pretty interesting working with them because, just about the time you've got them figured out, they do something different. I'll be telling somebody 'Oh, yeah, yeah, they do this and they do that' and then they'll do something totally opposite.

"We had some Canadian Indians down last Saturday. They're trying to get into raising buffalo and I was telling them different stories like that and finally one of them said, 'So the buffalo are teaching you again.'

"'Absolutely,' I said. 'They teach me something every day.'

"It's kind of full circle. Right now, it's our turn to take care of the buffalo. In the very near future, they'll be taking care of us again. In the past, you know, they totally took care of us.

"Humans have to be part of the management," Mike continued. "In the old days, we didn't call it management. We called it survival. We'd take X number of animals. Dealing with these animals, you know that at some point you're gonna have a surplus if you don't use them as they're meant to be used."

As everywhere in Montana where there are buffalo, the question of brucellosis must be handled on the reservation even though no sign of it has ever turned up here. While they do not vaccinate, every animal brought in is tested before being shipped in, tested again when it arrives, held until the results are back, then turned out with the herd. Every animal slaughtered in the field is also tested. Every test—which includes close to 100 documented kills and over 200 live animals the reservation has shipped out—has been negative. "That's our management plan," Mike says. "Just a hands-off, round 'em up once a year. Take what calves we need to get out of there. Turn 'em back. Till we get to the point where we can start a small slaughterhouse [a vision he has for a value-added industry on the reservation, one that might include a small store where tribal members can buy normally expensive buffalo meat reasonably]. Then management won't change that much because we'll still, hopefully, be shooting them in the field so we won't be chasing them, rounding them up. That'll be an even better improvement to the management plan."

We stood on a ramp along one side of the corral. I caught a sudden flicker of movement among the planks. A bird, I thought. A mouse. Maybe nothing, I decided. What would a mouse be doing up there? Then Mike said he'd seen something move and we both watched the planks. A ferret stuck his head out. It was such a tiny head! I wondered how he could possibly kill one of those big prairie dogs.

"They go down into the prairie dog burrows at night," Mike told me, I think relishing his story. "And lie down next to the sleeping dogs, then bite their necks."

It was afternoon when we left the corrals and the pastures to drive back to the gate. As we rounded Snake Butte, three bulls wandered among the boulders at its base, clearly a familiar place to them. They sidled up to specific rocks and began rubbing against them. One rubbed his shoulder back and forth and back and forth. I watched another rub his chest, up and down and up and down. He moved up slightly higher so the same rock was at stomach level, then rubbed his stomach, up and down. It seemed a little like something I shouldn't be watching. But I could see that they have been coming here for centuries; the rocks are so smoothly polished.

HORSE BUTTE

MIDAFTERNOON in late October; the sun hangs halfway down the sky. Our dogs run down the fine, steep black gravel bank to the narrow black beach edging Hebgen Lake. My friend Gena and I glissade after them. The dogs run along the strip of beach, in and out of water, over fallen old gray trees lying waterlogged, rotting into the beach. Near shore, the water moves in gentle ripples; farther out, in glassy streams of milk blue. Standing on the north side of the Madison Arm, we look across at Lionhead. It is a mountain I know. I've backpacked there, hiking up to the vast open meadows of its summit. It seems a long time ago, but all things seem a long time ago in the golden poignancy of autumn.

The lake was formed when Hebgen Dam impounded fifteen miles of the Madison River in 1915. The dam is strong. In 1959, it withstood a 7.1-magnitude earthquake centered on the region. On the lake's east side, Horse Butte Peninsula is embraced by the Madison and Grayling Arms. There is a fire lookout tower on the butte's high point. The peninsula is shaped like a beckoning index finger. Maybe that's why the buffalo come to it. Maybe they are being called.

Most of the peninsula is national forest, but of its six sections, two are in private ownership. Private land extends more or less from the middle of the peninsula to Grayling Arm, much of it laid out in numbered lots of less than an acre. A few other pockets of privately owned land in the region interrupt hundreds of miles of wild country—national forest and national park—extending in all directions.

We climb back to the top of the bank, then sit in the sagebrush on the flat between the lake and the dirt road we drove to get here. If we can be still enough, perhaps the crystal afternoon will not change. There is no sound anywhere. Not water lapping, birds singing, dogs barking; not us breathing. Absolute silence. The deep smell of sage takes the place of sound. A sudden pressing of wind against my ears comes as feeling, not sound. When a fish jumps and the sun moves down the sky, it is the beginning of time.

Horse Butte is about five miles north of West Yellowstone. The road to it turns off U.S. Highway 191, then leads straight through lodgepole pine forest into the residential development. From 191, you have no idea there is anything back there but forest. It seems an odd place to put a suburb. A fork in the road before the houses follows the line of the lakeshore. Signs on the hillside north of the road say the area is closed to protect wildlife, except where travel is permitted. It is permitted on a snowmobile road along the Madison Arm, up to the lookout tower, and on to the end of the peninsula.

Above the snowmobile road, tall dry grass weaves in and out of sage. Dried and whitened buffalo chips lie scattered over the ground. At the top of the hill, leafless gray aspen limbs form a lacy connection between the grassland and the dark fir forest beyond. From here, we cannot see the lookout tower or the signs or the road where we left the car. It almost seems a wild place.

In the residential area there are, along the periphery, a few houses that have been there since the mid-1970s. The larger number, a hodgepodge of manufactured homes and apartments among them, seem to have been put down any which way in the center of the area because somebody noticed the ground was flat. In this area, there is hardly a tree. It is open grassland, the kind of land buffalo like. On rolling, grass-covered hills northwest of the houses, cattle graze. Buffalo like that kind of terrain, too.

Horse Butte made the Bozeman paper almost daily during the winter of 1996–97 when the Department of Livestock was up there shooting buffalo. Residents interviewed complained about gut piles left lying along the road after dead buffalo were dressed and taken away. Buffalo they had been watching out their kitchen windows while drinking their morning coffee were being shot before their very eyes. Donna Lane, who worked as a bank teller in West Yellowstone and lived on Horse Butte, took it on as a cause.

119

A newcomer, she had arrived the previous June from Washington State.

"December first was a Saturday," she said to me in the first of our many phone conversations. "I got up about nine o'clock and went out to the kitchen to get water and saw a whole bunch of buffalo in the field. I watched them and was so excited and then, all of a sudden, I see three pickup trucks and six guys get out and kneel down and just fire and fire into the buffalo. They dropped every one of them. One got up and limped and they fired at him until he fell. There haven't been any cattle in that field for five years."

After that she began calling newspapers around the country, trying to tell America what was happening. "I feel there has to be a better way to resolve this," she said. "I want to get people involved."

She invited Montana Governor Marc Racicot, local and federal officials from agencies and organizations involved with wildlife, the local environmental organizations, the state vet, and the InterTribal Bison Cooperative to a meeting. "We live in the U.S. and we have a voice and if something isn't right, we have to form a group and let our officials know," she said.

When I spoke with her the day before the meeting she told me she had hired an attorney. "I'm being harassed by the local game warden," she said. "Thursday he made four different phone calls to my boss at the bank." She was told to balance her teller's window so she could go to the police station. "What have I done?" she asked. "All I've done is to deal with this bison issue and organize this meeting tomorrow."

She was called in as a "public nuisance," after the local sheriff accused her of putting hay out for bison along the Madison River the previous month. Route 191 crosses the Madison between West Yellowstone and Horse Butte, and bison feeding on the hay had caused traffic jams. Donna had not done it, although nobody ever found out who did.

Donna believed the real purpose of the call to the police station was to intimidate her. Determined not to let that happen, she began praying when she went to bed at night. "Lord, I know in my heart this is a good, strong thing." Perhaps it was her prayers, but she became more and more certain her role in relation to buffalo was ordained by God. Once she told me that God had directed her to save the buffalo.

On the morning of the meeting she was nervous. Although she was devoting most of her waking hours to the buffalo issue, and believed in the rights of ordinary people to be heard, I think she was surprised at how far her campaign had taken her. Far and fast. Media across the country were calling her. "Say a prayer for me," she said to me.

While some of the people she invited to the meeting came, Racicot was not among them. "I'm disappointed that the governor doesn't feel this is an important issue to sit down with the townspeople and talk about," she said.

There have been years of meetings about buffalo in Montana. The wonder is that so many people, on all sides of the issue, keep turning up. Yet if the organizations remain the same, the players change. People have gotten worn out by the issue; used up. They transfer out of whatever department they're in. They retire. They move to other states. A very few, like Jeanne-Marie Souvigney at the Greater Yellowstone Coalition, have stuck with it from the beginning. For Donna, everything that was happening was brand new. Some of her expectations were naive. So were some of her questions. But the power of the new is that few holds are barred because there is no history. When she asked whether the Board of Livestock would stop the killing if all buffalo were brucellosis-free, board chairman Jim Higinbarth of Dillon answered, "Yes." "Bullshit," Donna said.

Scott Carsley is one of the longtime residents on Horse Butte. A hunter, he was not particularly offended by the gut piles left lying there. He was, though, opposed to a lack of a solution. "This is just wanton slaughter," he said. "It is looking for an excuse to remove bison.

"There are a lot of Indians heading out to Horse Butte this morning," he said to me on the phone, meaning there would be some shooting. "Indians, trailers, livestock people, you see the government rigs, Fish & Game sometimes," Carsley continued. "It's quite a caravan."

To some of us it seems demeaning to call Indians in to do the butchering, but not the killing. It seems one more government handout; one more way to keep Indians in their place; one more way of not giving them back their buffalo. Bill Yellowtail called it "deeply insulting for game wardens to shoot buffalo and *give* them to the Indians.

"Dignity arises from self-sufficiency," he said, "Indians have to focus on that notion."

But those people who participate do so willingly, glad for the practical aspects of the dead buffalo. And in truth, what is most demeaning is for the buffalo to be wasted.

"I think the people as a whole would just as soon see Horse Butte set aside as a reserve for the bison," Scott Carsley said. "Some people would like to see a regular hunting season established. We have all these bison here and it's always disappointing to see them go somewhere else, but it's mandated by state law that they go to a charitable fund, or Indians. I have bison in my yard. I'd like to have bison in my freezer.

"There are more and more bison all the time and they're seeking traditional grounds. The truth of the matter is, we're the ones at fault here. We're building in their traditional grounds. It's the same old problem. Man encroaches on wildlife. They can blast all the bison they want, but next year there's going to be more."

Federal grazing land on Horse Butte has only one permittee, the Munns family from Idaho. Their permit is up for renewal on December 31, 2000. But the family owns private land up there, too, abutting their forest service allotment, so even if cattle were taken off the forest land, the problem is still not solved.

"It used to be," Keith Munns told me, "when the numbers were down in the park, we never did see a buffalo out there. And then it got where it was just 1 or 2 and then up to 20 and it's just getting worse and worse. This year, they've seen over 300. I really think it's a feed situation that spurs it on. We see those buffalo coming out of there in the fall, in October. There's too many of them coming out in the fall, and I think they're looking for feed."

The presence of buffalo has cost the Munns family money to test their cattle for brucellosis. "They know the threat's there and Montana State don't want infected cattle in there. None of us do, you know. But where I live in one state, graze in another, why the state rules we have to test those cattle, make sure they haven't picked the disease up."

A year earlier, Montana quarantined the Munns' herd, requiring testing before they could come off Horse Butte in the fall. It took about a week to pull the blood, process it, and get results back. Meanwhile, snow conditions threatened road closures. The Munns family feared that a week's time would get them snowed in, having to haul feed to the cattle. Feed is expensive. The family asked permission to move to their winter range in Idaho and test there, but the state would not allow it.

"From my standpoint," Keith Munns said, "it boils down to a couple of things—to have the threat of the disease, plus the destruction of fences and things like that. I think it all comes right down to the root of the problem is overpopulation."

Probably. But most likely not on the part of buffalo.

By late April 1998 warm spring days had urged new grasses out on Horse Butte. Lured by the fresh growth, between 150 and 200 buffalo wandered out of the park to graze. Rather than going in to shoot them, a hazing was organized. This was to be a cooperative effort, involving the

Department of Livestock, the park service, the forest service, the Gallatin County sheriff, and the Buffalo Field Campaign.

The Buffalo Field Campaign is an organization of volunteers who have vowed to keep buffalo from being killed. The core group is mostly young, living on very little in a communal existence and depending, quite literally, on the kindness of strangers. They have chained themselves to trailers hauling bison off to slaughter, blocked the road by erecting a manned scaffolding in the middle of it, trespassed on private land to haze buffalo to safety, gotten arrested over and over. With patrols out among the buffalo on Horse Butte 24 hours a day, they document every DOL action. (Cofounder Mike Mease, recording every action for a number of years, has produced a video—*Buffalo Bull*—that is an eloquent plea on the buffalo's behalf.) The volunteers have become responsible members of the communities where they live, devising innovative ways to help those communities. If buffalo damage fences, they fix them with no charge for labor, providing materials when they can. They have distributed BUFFALO SAFE ZONES signs to those people wishing to post their property. They offer a sort of "community 911 hazing service," as Mike Mease calls it, making themselves available to haze buffalo when someone needs them off their property. In spring, when buffalo gather along the road, the volunteers don orange vests (provided them by the police department) and warn motorists. Over CBs, they warn truckers.

When the late April hazing was organized, there was an edge of confrontation. The Department of Livestock let

Buffalo Field Campaign know that if its people got in the way, the DOL would start killing buffalo. Buffalo Field Campaign vowed to form a human shield if the Department of Livestock did start shooting.

April 28 was a warm, perfect day, one of those days when the air caresses you. Pockets of snow lay in the dark lodgepole pine forest on both sides of the road into Horse Butte. Beyond the road, the snow-covered peaks of the Gallatin Range rose into clear sky. Montana sky. A deep blue sky. Everyone was in a good mood. As if they were all going to a picnic. By the time I arrived at the parking area at the intersection of Route 191 and the road to Horse Butte, a journalist and a photographer from the Bozeman paper, a park ranger, a sheriff, a livestock inspector with a bushy mustache—who, the journalist informed me, apologizes to protestors before he arrests them—were standing around waiting for the buffalo to appear. The DOL and Buffalo Field Campaign seemed to have come to some sort of accommodation because nobody swaggered. A helicopter hovered over the lodgepole forest, searching for buffalo. It landed in the parking area, refueled, then resumed flying circles over the lodgepoles. Several vehicles carrying Buffalo Field Campaign volunteers came down the road to the parking area. They carried cameras to record whatever happened, but seemed eager for the chance to cooperate instead of protest. There were fresh buffalo patties on the road.

"They're bringing them down through the woods," one of the volunteers told me. "They'll probably come out down along the Madison."

I drove a short way down 191 until we were stopped by roadblocks set up in both directions. It pleased me that traffic would be officially stopped for buffalo. It had taken the buffalo ten thousand years to reach this moment when the DOL, the federal agencies, local law enforcement, and local activists were all working together to stop traffic for them.

I walked down toward the Madison following the hoofprints of buffalo pressed into the soft spring earth. Other people walked alongside me and in front and behind, all focused directly forward, as if they were alone, each of us as if we were alone. Walking in a dream. Following the footsteps of buffalo. Buffalo Field Campaign volunteers, park rangers, the journalist and photographer. Then, suddenly, we were all running as, well ahead of us, four bison came down out of the lodgepoles on the west onto the road and across and up into the trees to the east. The helicopter continued circling overhead. The main herd exploded out of the forest and down the slope to the road and up into the forest again on the east side. A cowboy on a horse shot a cracker rifle into the air. Three men on four-wheelers rode on the buffalo's heels and flanks, and the day erupted into shattering sound as the noise from the helicopter and the cracker rifle and the four-wheelers and the men's shouting all reverberated across the wild country. Like a heartbeat under the noise, under the earth, came the sound of 600 buffalo hooves running over the ground.

A young man on a bicycle followed them into the forest. A woman, who was too close as the herd came running, scrambled up a slender tree.

The buffalo moved out of sight, but the cracker shots continued. The roadblocks were removed. Traffic resumed. The young man on the bicycle returned, saying that once the buffalo were across the highway and into the woods, the hazers walked them. "So they wouldn't tire," he said.

The officials, who had not run down the road to be nearer the buffalo crossing, stood around one of the vehicles, waiting for information on the radio about six buffalo still in the forest. So far they remained hidden from the helicopter's view. The hazed herd, the radio reported, was hanging out by the river, a short distance inside the park. For the moment, everything in relation to them was on hold; everybody waiting to see which way they went before acting further. The search for the six in the forest continued.

A year later Mike Mease told me that, among those in the forest, were three old, wise cows. They hid not far from the road and bore their calves there. Two weeks later, unhazed, when their calves' legs were strong enough to go, they ran faster than any of the hazed buffalo had, up and down rises, across the road and into the park.

"Reminds you of the rat patrol," the mustachioed Montana livestock inspector said to a sergeant from the Gallatin County sheriff's office as they waited to hear about the six buffalo still in the forest. I stood nearby. Eavesdropping. "That's how you have to handle bison," he added, looking pleased. "Takes a little planning," he said. "Doesn't happen overnight."

"This seems to have worked well," I offered. "It looks like everyone worked together."

"This is not official," the livestock inspector said. "My personal opinion is—I don't care if they're there, but when people say they belong there, I'm not sure. The park is more like a drive-through zoo. The average tourist wants to drive through and see animals. To me, that's not what the park is about."

I didn't think to ask him what the park is about. Maybe in some way I agree with him enough that it wasn't necessary. Wildlife should not be on display. It should simply be. Yet we all crave connection with it. It's why we drive vehicles called Cougars and Rams and Eagles. It's why we call our school teams Bobcats or Grizzlies or Panthers or Hawks. It's why we wear shirts with wolves embroidered on them or buy paintings of lions and falcons. There are a hundred ways in which we take the emblem of a wild animal to represent us. We may think it's style, but, in fact, it's connection. "You are what you eat," my mother told me when I was little. So I wanted to eat bears. When, years later, I was finally offered bear meat, I ate it as a holy ritual, knowing what it was I took inside me, whose flesh I made my flesh. I feel the same way when I eat buffalo meat. We hunt because we identify with the animals we hunt. We are antihunting because we identify with those same animals. Any way you do it, you never get away from the connection.

So if wildlife has space enough to live, and if we can enter its space with respect and come away with wonder, with a sense of having been there, we make the connection. And if even the slightest memory of wildness flickers in us, the way a dream we almost remember flickers for an instant, we make the connection. If we do it from the road, from *inside* our vehicles, we are seen as far less threatening by the animal than if we walk up to it or encounter it by chance on a trail.

So maybe I disagree with the livestock inspector, after all. The park is, indeed, about entering a wild world—even if it's done from the antithetical safety of an automobile. Whatever works as a start, it is still about connecting. In being where elk live, where eagles and wolves live, where buffalo live, we share an instant on this earth. Who's to say there is a difference between an instant and eternity?

The sheriff and the DOL and the park rangers returned to the cleared area at the intersection of the Horse Butte road and 191 to work out a strategy for dealing—or, for the moment, not dealing—with those buffalo that refused to be hazed. The helicopter hovered over the lodgepole forest. The Buffalo Field Campaign volunteers scattered in their various directions.

In early June, by which time Horse Butte was fully engaged in spring, I flew over it on a Lighthawk flight arranged for the Greater Yellowstone Coalition's annual convention. Lighthawk, dedicated to flying environmental missions and monitoring land use, provides aerial support for groups engaged in environmental work throughout the Rocky Mountains, the Pacific Northwest, and, during the North American winter, in South America. Flying decision makers, grassroots activists, and the media over endangered lands, it provides them a literal overview of the problems.

The plane was a four-person Cessna, modified to handle flying over mountains during summer's turbulent air and to keep from disturbing animals. It has about 100 more horsepower than its original engine, and the quietest propeller the Lighthawk people could find. When it's flown with slow rpms, it is quiet enough for wildlife. The pilots maintain an altitude of at least 2,000 feet above people and animals. Pilot Reg Goodwin said that the quiet mode was "perfect for Lighthawk missions. We don't get shot at as much."

We took off from the West Yellowstone airport, which is not far from Horse Butte, heading south and east to fly over the park. Sitting in the copilot's seat, I had a view of earth primarily available to gods, birds, and pilots. Looking down on deep, shimmering snow covering peaks and high gullies and plateaus, on snow lying heavily on trees below the treeless summits, I saw earth wrapped in glittering, untouched silence. The shadow of the plane on snow looked like some great bird below us, determined to keep up. A herd of buffalo looked like ants.

Reg flew over Old Faithful and the Norris Geyser Basin, then turned north toward Mammoth. He took us over Blacktail Deer Plateau and the headwaters of the Gardner River; over the Yellowstone River and the flat bench area where the buffalo come out of the park to head up the Paradise Valley, the valley of the Yellowstone River. Flying between the Absaroka Mountains on the east and the Gallatin Range on the west, the valley seemed a funnel, a channel, a way for the buffalo to reenter the plains. Turning back, we curved around Electric Peak where wind-driven clouds merged with snow whipped from the summit into clear blue sky.

From the sky it's easy to see why buffalo come down to the valleys leading away from the park. Even the lower plateaus are still partially snow covered in early June. There is not a lot of comfort up there in a hard winter.

"You can see the park as a small area, flying over it," Reg said, "a finite area." Indeed, what would take weeks to cross on horseback takes minutes to fly over. What seems huge wilderness on the ground is a speck from the air, a tiny segment of the earth.

We headed back over Cougar Creek to Horse Butte. Below us buffalo capture pens built by the DOL on private land stood empty. These pens have hardly been used because most of the buffalo that made their way to Horse Butte were shot rather than transported to slaughterhouses. Since this flight, new pens have been built on forest service land, not far from an active bald eagle nest. Although the DOL is not allowed within 1,500 feet of the nest on motorized vehicles or on foot, they have driven snowmobiles up to about 100 feet of it. They have also driven snowmobiles along the Madison Arm open water during times of eagle feeding there.

We flew over cows on the grazing allotment, over a flock of pelicans on a tiny strip of land jutting into Hebgen Lake.

"That's my spirit creature," Reg said, looking down at the pelicans. For the moment, he forgot about buffalo. We flew past two groups of flying pelicans. They were on my side of the plane, and lower than us. "They'll all land in formation," Reg said, "touch down at the same moment. It makes the Blue Angels look like jerks."

Late afternoon in late October; the sun lowers behind the hills to the west. Rose-pink clouds hang softly in a pale blue sky. Gena and I and the dogs drive around the residential area on Horse Butte, curious what this place really is. A few people work in their yards. Three dogs play in a field. Two bull buffalo walk in the grassy fields between houses, as if the houses did not exist. As if only the buffalo and the autumn grass exist. One drifts up to the uncut grass around an empty house. He grazes below the porch. The other moves across the fields.

We head back toward the highway in twilight, coming upon one of the buffalo in the middle of a gravel road where it intersects the main road. Head down, he stands motionless. We drive up slowly. He is drinking from a puddle in the black gravel. Drinking from a puddle as if it were a stream. As if no road had cut these meadows. As if this were his world. His dark eyes are focused down, on the dark puddle in the dark road. Although he must sense the car, he does not move his eyes or his head or his body. We are not acknowledged. We are like the houses and the cattle and the signs and the roads. Newcomers at the end of 10,000 years. He does not look up as we pass.

PLAYING

FRED Donaldson is an old friend who turned up in Bozeman while I was working on this book. He came to present a workshop about play. He earns a living doing this; it is serious business for him. Learning about playing from children, Fred uses what they have taught him to continue to play with children. He plays with adults and with animals as well. As he understands play, there is no violence in it. For him, it is an experience in trust. In unconditional love. Children and animals do it naturally, he said. It is more difficult for adults.

I asked him if he had ever played with buffalo.

"Yes," he said.

"What was it like?"

"Like one face of God playing with another face of God," he said.

SING WITH THE
BUFFALO'S VOICE

ALMA Snell's house on the Crow Reservation faces a long
reef of red rock. The reef slants upward, rising as the land
rises. Above the red rock, a higher, bouldery ridge is covered by green vegetation and gray rock and lined with evergreens on top. On the red rims, there are only a few low
shrubs. Cottonwoods and willows fill the hollows between
the reef and the house. It is as if, from the deck of the
house, you can see the experience of this earth's history. If
you live in the house, it is what you know each morning
when you wake.

Behind the house, the hill climbs up to the sinking sun.
There are pines and firs on this side, and, in autumn, the
brilliant red of smooth sumac. It is red like fire, or a raw
place in the heart. Fading roses cling to long stems in the
garden.

I arrived at the house to meet Alma Snell on a cold, gray afternoon in early November. When Alma was a girl (she is now a great-grandmother), her father, George W. Hogan, was the keeper of the Crow's large buffalo herd. When I asked Alma over the phone if she would tell me stories about buffalo, she was noncommittal. She said she did not have the traditional stories; only stories from her own experience. But that was what I wanted. I already knew the traditional stories of how the buffalo had come to help the people. I wanted something more personal. When Alma hesitated about letting me come out to the reservation, I pushed a little because Putt Thompson, who runs the Custer Trading Post in Fort Smith, where the Snells live, said it would be good to talk to her.

I was greeted by a note tacked to the front door. Alma had gone to do a sudden errand. She said nothing about when she would be back. Ten minutes; two days; it could be anything. Rather than sit and wonder, I drove back to the main road and up to Yellowtail Dam, which is both nearby and a million miles away. The dam backs up the 71-mile-long Bighorn Lake to form the Bighorn National Recreation Area, managed jointly by the National Park Service, which handles recreational services, and the Bureau of Reclamation, which is in charge of water level.

Park service signs direct visitors to marinas and campgrounds and fishing sites. Visitor centers and paved roads and parking areas offer about 300,000 yearly visitors (the numbers vary according to weather and fishing conditions) the amenities they seek. Most of them never consider whose land this really is, or know that, up a gravel road a short way away, there is another world.

Below the dam, I took my dog to the Bighorn River so he could run a little. He waded into a shallow place for a drink. In every stream and river and lake we come to, he finds a place to enter for a drink. I think it's similar to my need to put my hand into rivers and streams: a sense of joining the movement of water; a way of becoming part of the stream; a private sort of baptism.

I returned to the house to continue waiting. Once, a long time ago in New York, I was late for a lunch date with a very rich man. (It took some extra time to get to a friend's apartment so I could borrow a suit to wear. The suit looked terrific.) When I arrived, he said, "Nobody ever keeps me waiting."

It's better to be in Indian country, I thought, where waiting is just a way of letting things happen in their own time. Waiting provides time you don't get otherwise. It's extra. It offers space to dream. Or to watch the rim rocks; to notice whether or not the earth shifts. If you are a writer, it is extra time to write. The rich man could have made important phone calls. He could have planned a seduction or a business deal or a safari. Waiting is open-ended time because you have no idea when it will be over. You can always leave, of course, but that way you'll never know what might have happened.

Alma arrived. I put away the notebook in which I had been recording the light and followed her into the house, carrying the herb plants I'd brought her, grateful the dog did not jump on them during the four-hour drive from Bozeman.

We sat down at the dining table, in front of a window looking out on the hill with the red sumac. Elderberries grow there, too, and probably a hundred other plants I cannot name. For Alma, the plants are as familiar as her children. It is what she does. She knows the plants that heal, and the plants that make tea, that add to the taste of food, that bring alive those things the Crow have always known. She learned these things from her grandmother, the medicine woman, Pretty Shield, whose life spanned the time of the buffalo to the time of change.

On the wall around the corner from the table there is a photograph of Pretty Shield. Collected in a single frame are separate photos of Pretty Shield and her husband, Goes-ahead, and of the German grandparents of Alma's husband, Bill. (The rest of Bill's ancestry is Assiniboine). In the frame, between the two sets of grandparents, is a single photo of Alma and Bill. They look good together.

Alma is the youngest of Pretty Shield's grandchildren. She is a joyous woman with steel-silver hair that frames her face in a mass of loose curls. (She told me that when Indian women first began getting perms, Pretty Shield wondered why they didn't just go rub their heads through the rose-bushes.) The deep lines around her mouth and at the corners of her eyes come from years of laughing easily, and the constantly animated way in which she speaks. Every part of her speaks. Her hands move; her head turns; her body indicates her words. It is as if she becomes each word, so that language and body are not separate.

She put on water for tea. When the tea was ready, she returned to the table to tell me about Lena, the Assiniboine aunt her husband, Bill, calls Mother. Lena reared Bill on the Fort Belknap Reservation.

When Bill Snell retired from his job with the Bureau of Indian Affairs, he and Alma moved from Fort Belknap to Crow. Sometime after that, Lena became crippled, requiring help, and the Snells returned to Fort Belknap. Bill told Alma she would have to take Lena when Lena wanted to go somewhere. "I'm afraid that she'll be wanting to look on at these places like she's used to doing," Bill said.

"She liked to go to powwows," Alma said.

Wherever Lena went, the cousin, whom she called her grandchild, also went. The girl, Joy Lynn, was 12 or 13 at the time of this story. One day Lena wanted to go to a celebration at Red Bottom on the Fort Peck Reservation, where she had relatives. "She used to love to go there," Alma said. "I made reservations at a motel and we went. We was in this big car. It was up to date and everything. That she always had. She always liked a new car. We had her wheelchair in the trunk. She sat on the passenger side and Joy Lynn sat in the back."

About five miles from their destination, a hailstorm struck. Alma, unable to see to drive, pulled into a turnoff to wait out the storm. "When the hail stopped, those cars were just almost one right after another on the road," Alma said. "They couldn't see. Even though their lights were on, you couldn't see their lights until they were about fifty feet. So they were moving very, very slow. That was what I was afraid of. Someone might be coming a little faster behind me. After they all passed and there was just one or two that was going by, it cleared up.

"We got back on the road and I didn't go half a mile when I looked up in the sky and there was," she paused for an instant, "a white buffalo in the sky. Pretty close. It looked like it was a male buffalo. It was angry. And it was not cloud-like. It was sketched like an artist would draw it. If it had any color to it, I thought, its eyes would have been red. The way it looked, just like it looked right at you. I looked at it for a while and I said, 'Lena, look at this!'"

Alma's voice took on an excitement as if she was, at that moment, seeing the white buffalo. It was as if Lena was sitting next to her in the car.

"She looked up as she was doing her rosary. 'Oh, my goodness, Alma, turn back! Turn back!' she said." Now Alma's voice took on an edge of alarm. It became a different voice from her own. It became Lena's voice. "'Something's terribly wrong here! Turn back! Look how angry it is!'

"I had no fear. It was there. It didn't move, like clouds would drift away. There was nothing but little puffy clouds here and there and the rest of it was blue sky, and this thing was in the air. I said, 'Lena, look at it. Look at the hooves. And look at the male parts of him. And look at the tail. Look at its horns, its nostrils. It's perfect . . .'

"'Oh, Alma,' she said, 'I don't want to go any farther. Turn back, Turn back.'"

142

I could hear the fear in Lena's voice.

"She was frightened," Alma said. "And she was for *real*. And I said, well, if that thing is going to stay there, I'm going to take a picture of it. So I got out my Minolta and I zeroed in on it and took about four pictures. Joy Lynn got out of the car and took pictures, too.

"And Lena said, 'Oh, my goodness, my goodness, I heard that'—and she mentioned a name I won't mention—'was conducting a Sun Dance and he must have done something wrong and he's angry.'

"Lena's dad was a pipe carrier for the Sun Dance all his life," Alma explained to me, "so that's why Lena is so close to whatever it means, the buffalo and its whiteness. We looked at it, and every time she looked, she'd cover her face away from it, and she'd say, 'Turn around, Alma, turn around!'"

As if she were Lena, Alma covered part of her face with her hands. She turned her head away from the buffalo, but left the farthest eye uncovered. She *became* Lena who could not look at this buffalo, while some part of her wanted terribly to see it.

"I said, 'Lena, we're just five miles from our destination. And I'm not gonna go back two hundred and some miles with you like you are, because you need rest. You've gotta have some rest before we turn back. I promise, I'll get you to the motel and you lay down and you rest a while and, if you feel like going back, we'll go back.'

"'All right,' Lena said.

"And I looked at this thing to disappear, to drift away, you know, like anything would. While I was looking at it, I didn't hardly even see it disappear. It was just—pfft—gone.

"I said, 'They won't believe me. They won't believe us until they see my pictures.' Lena said, 'Mmmmmmmmm-mmmmmm.'" Alma made a humming sound that seemed to come from somewhere deep inside Lena. "She just kept on going like that."

By the time the women arrived at the motel, a tornado warning was in effect. When Alma told me this, I naturally assumed the white buffalo had appeared as a kind of last vision for Lena; the angry sacred appearing on the edge of Armageddon. It all made sense to me and I prepared myself for some difficult denouement. The motel clerk told Alma they were, indeed, "riding the trail of a tornado," but assured her he would personally carry Lena downstairs if they felt it would hit. The women went to their room, where Lena lay down, although she could not relax. "She kept saying 'Mmmmmmmmmmmmmm,'" Alma said. "Every time she'd think of it, she'd make that noise. The little girl was already trying to get ready for the powwow. After the storm had gone, and the tornado missed us, and everything was kind of quiet, and people were moving around again and cars were moving around, I said, 'Lena, if you want to, I'll take you to the pow-wow grounds, and I believe that they will have it because it's nice now. The sun is out. And everything looks good again.'

"'I guess maybe we better, as long as we're here now,' Lena said, 'but I'm still thinking we should go back. Something might happen. Something terrible might happen.'

"I said, 'I don't think so, Lena. I don't think so. I'll take you over there and we'll talk about it.'

"So we went over there. The seats were empty because of the storm and everything, but the committee were trying to get the stand ready for the powwow. We had our choice of seats. There was no one around. They were probably still fooling with their lodges, whatever the rain didn't touch. I had to sit Lena right along the end of a row. I got pretty close to the platform so she could hear everything. She kept saying, 'Oh, my goodness, Alma, in *all* my long life'"— Alma's voice drew the words out longer, slower than her own natural speech, as if, indeed, Lena were speaking through her—"'I have never seen something like that. I have seen many things that were something to behold, but not that. I've never seen something like that before. I will never again see that. Ohhh, my, it was sooo angry. That buffalo was so angry.'

"I said, 'They say that white buffalo are. My people always say—my grandma, whomever I've heard—have said that the white buffalo were angry buffalo. They were mean. They stayed in the woods, mostly, if there was woods around. Stayed in the woods, in the shadows. Once in a while they'd come out and be with the buffalo, but on the edges of where they would roam. They don't really mingle with the rest of the buffalo. They were always loners.'

"Lena said, 'Ohh, if they're as mean as this one looks, they're *mean!*'

"And she couldn't forget it. In the meantime, a young man came. A young man came and was looking around. I noticed him because he had buckskin on. Buckskin jacket. His trousers were leather, but they were not a dancing outfit. It was just a wear. I noticed the buckskin and his hair being tied back, long. I thought how striking he was. He came and looked around. He was kind of pacing the platform over there. I looked at him and then I turned to Lena again and she was talking about how that buffalo shouldn't appear like that. 'It really does mean something, Alma, and I mean it. I believe these people did their Sun Dance wrong.'

"And this man came and sat next to me. Of all the seats that were empty, he came and sat next to me. He just sat there and looked on. He was kind of looking ahead. After a while he said, 'Is there something wrong?'

"I turned around to him and I said, 'My mother-in-law is bothered with an apparition that we saw of a buffalo, white buffalo, in the sky. More like in the air, really.'

"'Oh, you did?' he said.

"'Five miles from here. She can't get over it.'

"He said, 'How do you know it was a white buffalo?'

"I said, 'Well, the pencil . . . you would say the sketch of it was all white against the blue. You can see it. It was so plain. You can see every little tiddle of a buffalo. Of that buffalo. It was a male buffalo and it was looking toward us and it had these puffs coming out of its nostrils like it's mean. It was so disturbed. My mother-in-law couldn't look at it. Couldn't even look at it and wanted to go back.' I told him the whole story.

"He said, 'You did take pictures.'

"'Yes, I did. I took about four pictures of it and so did that little girl behind me.'

"'If those pictures come out, it's just a phenomenal thing that happened,' he said. 'And it really doesn't mean anything. But if they *don't* come out, it does mean something. And you will know one of these days.'

"We were so anxious to see the pictures. When I got mine, all the little puffs of clouds that were left way back were there, the blue sky was there. Where the buffalo was, it's just like you took your hand and swished it down. It had the white look erased. In the pictures, that is. But that's not the way it was.

"Four times. All the other pictures turned out perfect, of the pictures we took, but that four were the same *all* the way through. And when Joy Lynn's came back, her little camera took it, but it was the same thing. It wasn't there."

From that day on, Lena would not eat buffalo meat. "She just refused to eat the buffalo," Alma said. "She finally went to the rest home because she said she wanted to. I was lifting her and hurting my arm and everything else. My husband was a lot of help, but many, many times when I'd bathe her or something, it wasn't his . . . an Indian woman wouldn't allow her son to do that and maybe it's the same with all women.

"When she was in the rest home, people would bring her heritage foods, the way they fixed it over there in the Assiniboines, and they'd bring it to her and she'd look and she'd say, 'What kind of meat is this?' If they'd say deer, or beef, she would say okay, but if they happened to say buffalo, she wouldn't eat it.

"Bill says, 'Why is that? Just because she saw a buffalo in the air, how come she won't eat it?' She will not tell me the reason why, but she is sticking to it. I think what she feels is that it's too sacred to eat. Even if it is a different-colored buffalo (that people brought her to eat) and not the white one, which are very few, if any."

"But it came to you both as a vision," I said to Alma.

"It must have been a vision," she said, her voice lilting up like a song, and laughing at the same time. "You know, the girl saw it. All of us saw it. And at the time that this was happening, hardly a car went by."

"It's almost as if he waited for the three of you," I said, "because you said the whole line of cars had gone by."

"Mm-hm. After the storm they *all* moved on and we got on the road and we came about half a mile and then I looked up and you might say if I was walking, I stopped in my tracks. That's what I did. I applied the brakes. I said, 'Look, Lena,' and when I realized a car might be coming behind me, I went to the side so we would be safe in watching this thing. It's very strange, you know, then how they dream the buffalo, the white buffalo, and seeing them and all this stuff around. I hold it here," she said, touching her heart.

"I wanted to look more at it, because it was so absolute," Alma continued. "You see many imaginary things in clouds, but nothing like this one. He was facing east." Later, Alma asked an artist to draw the white buffalo. "Draw it like it's looking at you, angry," she said to him. "And make it face east."

148

The artist tried to make the drawing, but could not. "I cannot draw a buffalo facing east," he said to Alma, finally. "I can draw it the other way. I've tried, but I'll try some more and if I ever get it, I'll bring it back to you so you can have it."

There was laughter in Alma's voice as she recounted the artist's struggle.

"It's from the east that the destruction happened to the buffalo," I offered. "It's where it all came from. No wonder the buffalo was angry."

Alma laughed again, this time at my earnestness. "I never thought of that," she said, still laughing. How much more easily she accepts the presence of the buffalo, I thought, than I do.

"But that's one thing we saw that was sort of an extraordinary thing that did happen," Alma said. "I've never seen it again."

Alma looked out the window toward the hillside, now soft in dusk. She said some people had seen a white buffalo in the woods at the top of the hill. "They went up above and they were hunting and then they saw this buffalo coming sort of from that canyon direction, this way. And they said, 'Look!' And they said they shot at it. And I said, 'What did you shoot at it for?' They said, 'I guess we wanted to be the ones to take that white buffalo. We'd have it stuffed, or something, and keep it. Because if we don't, somebody else would get it.' That's what they told me."

"But isn't the white buffalo sacred?" I asked.

"Hmmm," she said, matter-of-factly.

"And is it all right to shoot at something that's sacred?"

"I don't know. To the Sioux, especially," she said, answering my first question.

"Not so much to the Crow?"

"I've never really heard about it. But the Sioux do say it's sacred. My mother-in-law is Assiniboine, so she's Sioux, so maybe that's why it disturbed her so much. 'Cause to me, it was absolutely a beautiful sight because it was so much like a male buffalo. Its tail was right straight out, with the brush, the bushy part on the end, right straight out like it does when it gets mad, the buffalo. Even that was there.

"My dad would always sing to us. 'Buffalo, buffalo, *cheesh du shia.*' That means curly tail," she translated for me. "But when it gets mad it must get straight out, because it had a straight-out tail," she said, laughing.

Alma's father stayed with the buffalo on Windy Point. "My father stayed in that place and he stayed there all winter long, watching these buffalo. He used to tell what their habits were. He said, one time they got out, out of their territory, out of their fence. He told me that he was helpless. He thought—ohh, there go all the buffalo. They'll scatter everywhere. So he said he went out and walked among them. He walked among them and he sang. Indian songs that he would remember. And he kept singing them, kind of low. Not loud, but kind of low. 'They were grazing,' he said, 'but when I got to the leader and started singing and coming over toward the way, the leader followed.' It followed him. He kept on singing and going on and went on into the gate that he had opened and the leader went on in there with him and all the rest came. *All* the rest came. 'And that time,' he said, 'I almost lost all them buffalo.'

"He just went on in and closed the gate and he said, 'I was so happy.' What songs he sang, he didn't say, but he said, 'I sang to them in a low voice and kept on and went over to the leader and came on and he followed me.'"

"Do you remember when your father took care of the buffalo?" I asked.

"I went up there to visit him. He used to try to be with us as much as he could after my mother died. He used to sing to us. Lullabies."

"Maybe the lullabies he sang to the buffalo," I said.

"Maybe, maybe, I bet it was. He kept his voice low, like their voices, and he got them in there. They followed him."

After a moment in which the dusk deepened; a moment of crescent memory, Alma said, "He shouldn't have gone among the buffalo. They're dangerous!"

"But didn't you feel proud of his bravery?"

"Oh, yes, I thought, my dad is a brave, brave man to do that. And he is so loyal to his tribe that he just didn't want those buffalo lost. He didn't want them to scatter everywhere and the tribe won't have anything. He had to do something. I imagine he prayed. He's a praying man, you know. And he must have prayed and he went out there. And he sang to the buffalo. And he finally got to where the leader is and he started going, singing, and the leader followed and all the rest came with him, and they went into the pasture and he closed the gate. Oh, my, Dad, you *did* this and we weren't even around to rescue you if something did happen." She paused for an instant, thinking. "I guess sometimes they do come after people, you know."

"If people intrude on their space," I said, "but your father wasn't doing that. He was simply *being* with them."

"A part of them, like," she said.

It was full night now. I could no longer see the hillside or the smooth sumac, the autumn colors or the edge of sky. I sipped my tea. I wondered if it was time to go, but then Alma began to talk about listening to the women her grandmother's age talk about buffalo. "They'd laugh about it, the parts that they took, what they did with them and everything. But I'll tell you something else, too, that an Assiniboine lady told me in these little tidbit stories that they tell in their remembrance of buffalo. She said that when the buffalo was skinned out and women went to work on the sections, she used to go up to the hump and sort of pound on it, pound on it and rub it, sort of rub it toward the end where the head was. She said there was a kind of a little hole there, kind of finger size, and that's where the fat came out of. From there she had a little container she would put under there because the fat that dripped out of there was unsaturated. Emma Lame Bull was her name. She's gone now."

"Is that still done?" I asked.

"It's never been done that I know of, except then," Alma said. "I've never seen my grandmother do it," she continued. "The only thing she does that I know of that's fat, other than what's on the flesh, was the bone, the marrow. She loved to give us that so we could eat it. Oh, I loved it.

"I haven't had buffalo slaughtered in front of me and skinned and everything and taken the head off to find out where it would be either," she said. "I've never had that experience. But they said they do, Emma and her family."

We had been sitting in front of the window a long time. My tea was gone. Alma's, barely touched, must have been cold. She took a little sip, a gesture that brought me back to the table. I had been so fully in some other place; on Windy Point with her father; on some vast prairie on Fort Belknap with Emma Lame Bull; watching the sky for the white buffalo. Alma took another sip of cold tea and began telling me about her trip to Ted Turner's ranch near Bozeman.

As a recognized authority on plants and their uses (when I visited, she was at work on a book about plants, especially medicinal plants, and her experiences with them), Alma was among a group of archaeologists and other experts invited to explore what the huge acreage where Turner runs buffalo holds. Her daughter, Faith, drove from Crow to the ranch with her.

The ranch road passed through a locked gate to the cabins where the group was working. Approaching the gate, the women drove through buffalo. "Oh, *my*, you just couldn't count them," Alma said. "They were just like a sea of buffalo. It was fascinating for me to see that. I thought, this is the way it used to be."

When a man who worked for the ranch appeared in a pickup, Alma and Faith stopped to talk with him. He pointed out their way, then said, "I have never seen these buffalo come to this gate all together—the whole herd. They're in patches. There's always *some* here, a lot of them here, but for the whole herd to come to this place at this time, I don't know what's going on."

"Do you think they knew whose daughter you were?" I asked.

"That's what he was thinking," Alma said. "We just went through them buffalo and we could stick our hand out of the rolled-down window—if our windows were rolled down—we could touch them as they were grazing. They just kind of *moooved* slowly to one side and we just went through them. I got to the gate, and I had a combination.

"Faith said, 'What are you going to do? There's buffalo all around us.'

"I said, 'I know, I have to open that gate.'

"'Mom, I'll leave the door open.'"

Alma laughed, saying, "If they got mad, this car wouldn't mean a thing to them. I got out slowly and I walked over to the gate and I got the combination and then I would pull it. Nobody ever told me that you have to push the lock together so it would snap open. So I'd get it to the number and I'd try to jerk it down and I thought, *what* am I doing wrong, and all these buffalo around. I was a little bit within my own self. I didn't want to show no fear.

"And then, here was a little calf right against the hill where the gate was, and this was a drop-off. This little calf was having a fit over there—maaaaaaaa . . ." Turning her head one way to see the calf, she imitated its bawling. "And this mother cow was over here." She turned the other way to see the mother buffalo. I followed her movements, as if the animals were present.

"'Oh, Mom . . .'

"'Don't holler, Faith.'

"About the third try I thought I'd go back and find that guy, wherever he went. I said, in Crow, to this little calf, 'You quit bellering around. Your mother's getting nervous. You go on over there. Who's going to bother you anyway? Go on over to her,' I said. And I looked at that mother and that mother was kind of anxious for her little one. Then the calf went right behind me and went over to this cow. The cow kind of nudged it around a little and they turned to go that way a little ways, then she stopped and looked back at me, like this." She turned her head over her shoulder now, imitating the cow looking back at her. There is acknowledgment in the cow's eyes. It is there in Alma's eyes. Two women. Mothers. "And she turned around and she went," Alma said.

"So I tried the lock again and I happened to just hit it. It snapped open. I opened the gate and I had to push some of those buffalo a little bit, so I did it real easy. They moved out of the way and Faith came through and I had to close it again. I pulled that gate closed and locked it. And boy, that car might not mean a thing to them, but I was sure glad to get in it.

"Faith says, 'Mom, you're not even scared.'

"And I say, 'You don't know what goes on inside.'

"Anyway, we went on and she says, 'Mom, I have never seen so many buffalo together in all my life.'

"I said, that's the way they looked. Bill's grandmother used to tell me that they used to look *way* off, and they'd see a black patch and they looked like a burnt-out place. They would always put a stick in front of the head of the patch, and if that black went beyond, it was buffalo *way* off. 'And then we'd start moving toward it so we could have meat,' she said.

" 'Faith,' I said, 'this is the way it was. Just like a great burnt-out place on the prairie.'

"We went over to the cabin and did our work. The buffalo were scattered everywhere. They were in bunches all over the place. The morning we were supposed to leave, my daughter woke me up. She said, 'Mama, them buffalo are all here again.' I said, 'How do you know?' She said, 'I looked out my window and they're at my window and I looked outside and there they were. They were grazing.'

"And the cook said, 'My golly, they came to bid you good-bye.'

"And so that whole herd was there and my picture was taken with them." She laughed again.

"You laugh at that," I said, "but do you not believe that actually happened?"

"Well, to me it could have been coincidence."

"It could be," I said, "except I don't believe that anything on earth is coincidence."

"You don't . . ." she said, laughing again at my non-Indian intensity so that I could not help but laugh with her.

"So we saw the buffalo," she said, "and we were very happy that we could see buffalo roaming around, and free."

THE BUFFALO IN YELLOWSTONE

IN the valley below us hundreds of buffalo move back and forth across the high alpine meadow, an inexorable force breaking upon the shores of time and of place, the whole restive herd shifting with the urgency of the bulls' drive. August. The rut. The bulls' bellowing roar rises out of the dust as they run one way and then back and then back again like something crazed and craving. The roar is like the sounds of lions, of oceans, of heaven ripped apart by thunder that does not end.

Bulls chase cows; chase other bulls. Calves, some new enough to still be red, run along with their mothers. Bulls sink suddenly to the ground in wallows; roll; rise again spraying up soft sand like some discolored morning mist.

The air has an edge to it. It is no longer entirely summer. The buffalo know what time it is, what season, what need. We know it, too—Dick, the outfitter; me, the guide;

the guests we have led to this place. Sitting here on top of the Mirror Plateau, watching the buffalo cross and recross and cross again the deep green meadow, all of us feel the coming of autumn.

The Mirror Plateau is part of the rim of the Yellowstone caldera. Forming the northeast corner of the caldera, it extends across an area between the Lamar and Yellowstone Rivers, rising high above the surrounding country. We had ridden two days to reach it, through Pelican Valley and up Astringent Creek, over the divide to Broad Creek, then back and up the nether reaches of Pelican Creek to the Mirror.

This is grizzly country and elk country and country of the buffalo. The hidden buffalo. The ones you do not see from the road. They move across these high pastures all summer. There is good grass with high protein up here. Abundant good grass.

Approaching the Mirror from inside the Yellowstone caldera, we sit on the plateau about 200 feet above the buffalo, which move across a large, sloping grassland edged with trees. Toward the height of the meadow, trees and pasture mingle, forming a park. Now and then a buffalo moves into the trees, then reappears higher up on the pasture as if wanting no part of the relentless rampage that fills the sky with roaring and the vibrating thunder of so many hooves running crazy over the grass.

There is as much ritual to this display as there is to any other sexual event. The ritual is integral to the event; fundamental to all those things that form the core of our beings—the sexual, religious, political things—the things we are instructed never to discuss over dinner. These, the matters of life importance, are not to be entered without ceremony. Ceremony is instinctive. It is the presentation of hope; the ordering of nature.

The bull sniffs and licks a cow's genital area, then, extending his neck, he raises his upper lip slightly, rolls his eyes back, and stands motionless for a few seconds.

What is this to a buffalo? To a voyeur, it seems an ecstatic moment.

The bull stays close to the cow, trying to keep other bulls away. Receptive to him, the cow may suddenly take off into a run the instant before he would mount her. The tease. He chases. Other bulls pick up the excitement of the chase until a parade of bulls, one after another after another, runs through the herd.

On other trips into the Mirror, we have seen solitary bulls, or groups of two or three bulls along the way. They are everywhere. In Pelican Valley where we start; on Broad Creek; in the meadows below the Mirror. When a buffalo is on the trail, we circle away, riding far below or above it. We do not interfere with the buffalo's space.

You cannot trust the buffalo will see you first and move out of the way. They do not have particularly good eyesight, although, if we are upwind, they can smell us, the horse smell and the human smell of us. They can hear us, hear our voices, the movement of our horses. But sometimes we are near enough for them to see, and then they watch us. They hardly move as they watch us.

Earlier, riding through a narrow isthmus of grass that curves slightly as it delivers us from one meadow to the next, we saw a big bull on the outside of the curve. He watched us coming. As we rode into the curve, a group of seven or eight bulls became visible at the edge of the woods on the inside of the curve, the side on which the trail passes. We moved out into the center of the curve. I wondered if the big, solitary bull would think we were moving in too close. I kept my eyes on him as we rode. He kept his eyes on us, his head moving slightly to take us all in; Dick leading, pulling his three mules; me behind him, pulling my three mules; our ten guests behind me.

I hoped no one felt the urge to stop for a photo. I hoped my lead mule, Buck, felt no urge to move out to the side for that better piece of grass he always sees somewhere out there. I hoped the buffalo understood we were only passing through. He could move in such a flash of a second—a "hot second," Don Meyers said when I visited him at Rocky Boy's. I wondered if a buffalo can hear a human heart beating. I wished I knew less about buffalo. I wished I could simply look at him this close in wonder and pass by easily.

In the warm afternoon, we sit on the inner edge of the Mirror Plateau, leaning against fallen logs, eating lunch. We rode about 5 uphill miles to get here and the horses are glad of the rest. The buffalo herd was here when we arrived. They are still here when it is time for us to leave. To continue our route back to camp, we must cross the buffalo meadow.

"Can't we go below them?" I ask Dick.

A broad swath of high green grass lies between the bottom of the Mirror and the hillside where the buffalo are. It looks to me as if we could cross it to the trees on the right, then climb up and over the hill through the trees, way to the right of the buffalo.

"It's all boggy there," he says.

"Can't we go back the way we came?"

"But we're going up *there* . . ." he says, pointing to a high ridge to the west of the meadow.

The way we came would take us in an entirely other direction. Of course, it would still work. We *are* going back to the same camp. But it would not complete the circle of our day.

Half a dozen elk appear on the east side of the meadow. They do not come down to mingle with the buffalo, but graze their own way on the side hill where they stand.

"We'll go above them," Dick says.

I wonder how we can do that without going through them. They have spread out, but suddenly close in together, forming a circle. This is normally a protective act, with the calves and the yearlings on the inside. In the circle, they move clockwise, up the pasture.

We look for a bear or wolves or something that would change their random running into so organized a pattern, but see nothing. As suddenly as they circled and moved, they settle down again, resuming their earlier activity. The bellowing of the bulls spreads, again, across the meadow.

"I don't really want to go past them," I say.

"They are defensive animals, not offensive," Dick says.

"But they may see this many animals [twelve horses, six mules, twelve riders] as a threat from which they must defend themselves," I say, knowing full well there is not much point in objecting. We will go the way Dick says we will go. At least I have the comfort of knowing he knows what he's doing. He is not burdened by the extremes of caution that are in me. He is less fearful than I am, far more sure of his ability on a horse. With reason.

Meaning to somehow reassure me, Dick says, "I don't want to disturb them."

"They are already agitated," I say, not in the least reassured.

"But not by us," Dick says.

Mounting our horses, I pick up my mule string and try to visualize how to act if a buffalo should charge. I am not successful at this. We start down the hill. The buffalo run up the meadow and disappear over the ridge. They must have known all along we were there. They must have been waiting for us to make a move.

They are gone over the ridge. There is no dust from wallows, from running hooves. If we had arrived at the top of the Mirror at this moment, we would never have known they were here.

Over a hundred buffalo, and we would never have known.

We ride from the pine-fir forests and open meadows of Coyote Creek across the Hellroaring bridge, down to the Yellowstone River, across a desert landscape of sagebrush and cactus, heading west to the confluence of Crevice Creek with the Yellowstone River. The Crevice Creek trail is no longer maintained and we miss it, riding a mile downriver before realizing we have gone too far. It is already late.

Dick has been to Crevice Creek before. The rest of us, the other wrangler and I and the eight guests, are just following with no idea what we are looking for. When Dick turns his horse to head into a thicket of trees and shrubs that he sees, somehow, as a trail, I am certain he cannot be right. Yet, once through the tangle of green, there is, indeed, the remnant of a trail. A very steep trail. Overgrown, it disappears beneath shrubs and fallen trees and the debris of seasons, reappearing just often enough to keep us more or less on it. The horses literally pull themselves up, us leaning far forward to help to the extent we can. I think about riding back down. I try not to think about riding back down. It is dark here; dark in the thick forest anyway; dark as the day's light fades. We climb into evening, into night. When we arrive in the high meadow where we will camp, it is full night.

We set up camp in the dark. Dick cooks by the light of a Coleman lantern and people eat without much conversation. They are tired. We are all tired.

This trip is one that I am, nominally, leading. It is a Yellowstone Institute course, one of many the Institute, the educational arm of the Yellowstone Association, offers summerlong. Dick, whose Ph.D. is in botany, is the Institute's horsepacking outfitter and the usual teacher on the trips we do. On those trips, I am just a wrangler.

Each trip has a theme. On this one, it is our connection to wild country, a connection we explore through various exercises and writing, which is why it's my course and
not Dick's. Except that it takes place in wild country, it is
not unlike the occasional writing workshops I conduct.
Once in a while somebody comes on one of these trips who
is actually interested in writing. And sometimes there are
even people interested in exploring their own connection
with wildland. Mostly, though, I think people don't bother
reading course descriptions. They see the word *horsepacking*
and sign on.

At Crevice Creek I had planned time in which each of
us would sit—entirely alone—in the night meadow for 20
minutes. Twenty minutes alone in a wild meadow in the
dark of night could be an eternity. More often, though, it is
entrance into the eternal. Even those people for whom it is
at first unnerving are almost reluctant to come in by the
time I bring them back. They have truly entered into the
night, incorporating its sounds and smells and air and dark
and stars into themselves; become creatures of the night-
time wild. Being called back is an interruption.

This, however, was not the night to do this. All of us
had already had as much experience of night as anybody
wanted.

It is hard to come into camp late; hard to add extra
miles of getting lost to the long miles that most Yellowstone
trips automatically entail. A few people see it as challenge;
as adventure. Most people, dead tired, just want their sleeping bags.

For the outfitter and the guide, it is not easy feeling you have caused guests discomfort. They trust you to get them there, and then you miscue, and you feel you have failed them. In reality, you have presented a little slice of actual wilderness travel, a place made up of the unknown, but so few of us consider reality when we are deeply tired. When the trip is over, even those who were frightened or overtired usually recall whatever it is—getting off trail, weathering a storm, getting too late a start and so, too late a finish—as adventure. Some kind of high point. But not now. Not at the end of such a day.

We sleep heavily, deeply. We wake to clear dawn in a high meadow filled with flowers. Crawling out of our tents, we finally arrive in this place. It is fresh with the crystal cool of summer morning. It is like arriving on the earth for the first time. We are not alone. Above us, in the high grass, in the wildflowers, there is a buffalo, his presence a benediction.

In early June, the Yellowstone ranger staff holds a meeting of the outfitters and guides who work in the park. It is a time for the rangers to present any new or changed regulations; an orientation for new guides; a certification of all guides for the coming season. It is also a chance for guides and outfitters to get together with rangers with whom, one way or another, they work all summer.

A ranger reads the required information to us, then asks if we have questions. At the June meeting a few years ago, one man wanted to know if there are prescribed methods for handling bison in the trail when there is no way to go around them. "Throwing stones at them usually works," the ranger suggested.

A month and a half later, Dick and I and twelve guests ride up the Pelican Valley, en route to the Mirror Plateau. A couple of miles from the trailhead, the trail descends a hill, crosses a bog, and immediately climbs a much steeper hill. There is a short, curving path across the bog. If your horse steps off the path, he will sink into God knows what. Horses or mules caught in such a place can sink all the way. At the very least, they face a terrified struggle. You do not want your horse taking a step off the trail here. If you get off your horse and step into the bog, exactly the same thing will happen to you.

The path across the bog ends with the first step up the hill. Although the hill is long and dry, this is the only place you can get up it without stepping into the oozing, black-green muck. Once you have committed to crossing the bog, there is no room to turn around.

We ride down the first hill and begin crossing the bog when three bull buffalo appear on the hill we are approaching. Dick's horse is at the bottom of that hill, his mules strung out behind. I and my mules are all on the bog trail. A couple of riders are, too; the rest remain on the dry hillside we have just descended. The buffalo walk down the hill toward Dick. They stop about halfway down, directly on the trail.

Dick stops his horse. We all stop. We cannot go forward. We cannot back up. (There is no way to back up a string of mules.) We cannot get off to gather up stones as the ranger suggested. Besides, I don't like that idea anyway and say nothing about that suggestion to the people who are still on dry land. How do you *know* the buffalo will run away instead of getting mad? Buffalo that have had enough have been known to stomp the hoods of cars, for heaven's sake. Who are we to judge when a buffalo has had enough?

Dick looks toward the side of the hill to the right of the trail. Because there is nothing that he cannot make his way up or down, everything always looks possible to him. I suggest we wait. Grazing buffalo, after all, don't stay in one place for terribly long. Not that waiting is the best thing to do, either, because the horses, used to being allowed to eat by their guest riders, are apt to decide the bog grass looks pretty good. They can easily graze into the bog, if their riders are not paying strict attention. And the riders are paying no attention to the horses because they are all looking at the buffalo. In any case, the mules, which eat their way down all trails, will certainly graze into the bog.

The buffalo, meanwhile, are not grazing. They are just standing on the trail. They know perfectly well we want to ride up that trail. They are not about to move. They watch us.

The plains tribes have stories about the man who married a buffalo. These are stories about how the buffalo test us. They tell how the buffalo try the courage and sincerity of the man who married one of them. I wondered if the buffalo on the trail were a test. Or if they simply had a point to make. I don't know if buffalo make conscious decisions and probably I should not even suggest that they do, but they were certainly making their point.

The guests do not speak. They are as riveted on the buffalo as the buffalo are on us. After a long time, when the buffalo have let us know what they want us to know, the big bull in front of the other two moves slowly off the trail, slowly up hill. The other two follow. They do not rush.

We ride up the trail after them, understanding what we have been taught.

My first trip to Yellowstone was in the winter of 1982. A magazine had sent me to Montana to write a ski story and, after spending a couple of days at Big Sky, I was invited to join a group snowmobiling the 30-mile trip from West Yellowstone to Old Faithful. I arrived a bit late at the snowmobile shop to find the group had gone on. The shop owner outfitted me with a snowmobile, a modicum of instruction, a suit and boots, and the information that I would find the group at Old Faithful.

With the suit on, I walked like the Goodyear blimp. I looked like it, too. I wondered why so many people, women especially, like to snowmobile when it makes them look like this. Better to ski. At least you look good when you're standing around. I thought I would have to be hoisted onto the snowmobile. The man told me I would adjust.

I more or less got the hang of driving the thing as I rode through the town streets to the park entrance. Once there, I had the road to myself. (At that time there was relatively little snowmobile use of the park, although the road from West Yellowstone to Old Faithful was groomed for the machines.) I fiddled around with speed to show myself I could, indeed, speed up or slow down at will. Because the machine made less noise at slower speeds, and vibrated less, I did not drive very fast. It was nice not to have the noise of other snowmobiles and I was quite pleased with myself for having had the foresight to be late. An eagle flew across the road in front of me. I passed a small herd of elk in an open space.

At Old Faithful, I parked near a short row of snowmobiles, slowly slid off the machine, and even more slowly waddled over to the geyser. According to the sign, it was scheduled to go off in about ten minutes. There were three other people there. I sat down on a bench and waited.

It erupted as growing bursts of hot steam against the gray, cold, afternoon sky; sputtering and bursting in higher and higher explosions of steam. Droplets of water fell out of the steam like little, separate jewels, hitting the bare ground surrounding the geyser. Then, used up, the water fell back on itself until nothing more came out of the earth.

I have since watched Old Faithful many times, but always in summer when hundreds and hundreds of people gather in front of it. Once I was there when it erupted against a full moon. There were not many people in front of it then, and night made it seem like some secret event. But never, watching it, have I witnessed so wild an act of nature as on that gray winter afternoon when four of us sat to watch.

I stopped long enough to have a sandwich at the Snowlodge and to look around for a group of people I might belong to. How would I know? All the other people were in groups. All the groups looked alike. Everybody in them looked like walking inner tubes. I decided to forget about the group. I'd enjoyed my ride *to* Old Faithful alone. I'd enjoy my own ride back.

The Fountain Paint Pots are almost halfway between Old Faithful and Madison Junction. I liked the name and wanted to see them. I climbed off my snowmobile (I was getting better at this) in the parking area and started down the half-mile-long boardwalk that weaves among the delicately colored mud pots. The mud pots are formed when sulfuric acid dissolves rock into mud in a place where there is not enough boiling water deep beneath the surface to make a geyser or a hot spring. On the surface, the boiling mud is colored lovely shades of blue and rose and yellow and gray. It bubbles and pops, sometimes throwing mud bubbles into the air. It is color and sound and movement all at once, a quite extraordinary show the earth produces.

I waddled down the boardwalk that curves to return you to the parking area. It seemed to me no mean feat to walk half a mile in that suit. Every step must be a deliberate decision; otherwise the suit takes over, and you would plop down. With less grace than a mud bubble. As I approached the end of the boardwalk, a buffalo walked down a slight rise to the left of it, onto it. I had never seen a live buffalo before.

He stood on the boardwalk, not quite facing me. I stopped, fascinated, vaguely frightened. It seemed to me that I should do something. The animal was huge. Gorgeous. Awfully near. I wondered what it was I should do. I wondered if he was coming my way. If he was going *any* way. I wondered if, seeing me, he would turn around and go back up the hill. I wondered whether, if he did, it was safe to proceed down the boardwalk. The buffalo remained motionless. I could see the parking area beyond him. I was so close to it. I hated the idea of turning around to waddle half a mile back the way I had come. I turned around.

In the parking area I climbed onto the snowmobile and drove the rest of the way back to West Yellowstone. I had seen my first buffalo. I had been turned back by my first buffalo. I hated my snowmobile suit.

I had been living in Montana for a few years when one bright winter morning I packed lunch in my rucksack and drove down to the park. The road from Mammoth to Cooke City, the only road in the park plowed for vehicles other than snowmobiles, affords access to some lovely skiing. Parking at one end of the trail across Blacktail Deer Plateau, I put on my skis and started out. Open and easy and gorgeous, this is the perfect place for me to ski.

A weekday, there was no one else around. Skiing like that makes you feel you own the world. Or you discovered it. Or you are integral to it. It is a powerful feeling; full and serene.

Even so, you get hungry. I began looking for the perfect lunch spot. For me, that means something to lean against, facing the sun. A few yards down the trail, off trail to my right, I noticed a large, snow-dusted boulder. Sun hit its far side. My place, I thought. I could lean against the boulder, be warmed by the sun in front, sheltered by the boulder in back, laze away an hour on a spectacular day, ski a little more, and go home.

I skied toward it through soft, glittery snow where mine were the first tracks. When I was about 10 feet away from my boulder, it got up and walked away.

Buffalo, sleeping in the sun.

On a mid-September trip into the Mirror Plateau, Dick and I and four guests leave the Pelican Valley trailhead with a storm-dark sky behind us and late day around us. The meadow grasses are bright gold. Except for an occasional fading aster, the flowers are gone. Although it is warm, it is fully autumn. Beyond the bog and the Pelican Creek crossing, a bull buffalo stands in the trail. He seems a lone bull but, as Dick moves forward, we see a herd of about 10 bulls in a little cove on our left that had been blocked by Dick and his mules. We swerve off the trail to the right, returning well past the first bull, which has not moved.

The storm sky moves toward us like a blanket being pulled up the sky. We worry about being caught by night in these now short days. Night and storm.

Before Astringent Creek, we notice a dark animal higher up the valley. Lately, I always think "buffalo" when I see a distant animal. (In Pelican Creek, which is prime grizzly habitat, every form *used* to be a bear. But we all change obsessions from time to time.) The animal moved wrong for a buffalo. Bear, maybe. Wolf.

"Wolves," Wolf Schroeder says, looking through his binoculars. He counts ten of them.

We are taking Wolf, his former wife, and their two grown children to the Mirror Plateau. Wolf is the director of the Munich Wildlife Society and a wildlife biology professor at the University of Munich. He wants to go see if the wolves have a kill site there, but we got a late start on this trip and, halfway to camp, are running out of light. Because we will return this way, we decide to check out the site on our way back.

Wolf knows the wolves of Europe; the wolves of everywhere, probably; he knows the European bears in ways that seem enormous to me now, so parochial have I become as an American. I remember once walking a mountain trail in Tyrol and coming upon an engraved metal plaque that said, ON THIS SPOT THE LAST BEAR IN TYROL WAS SHOT. I don't remember the date, but it was a long time ago.

What Wolf knows is that wildness and civilization can coexist; each adapting to the other. We do not know that in America. For us, everything is a fight; everything *must* be one way or the other.

The following day, on our way to Broad Creek, we pass a lone bull, huge, unmoving. He stands off to the side, facing us. A deep black-brown, his coat is full and glossy, ready for winter. I can see him watching us, but nothing moves. Not his head, not his eyes, not his tail. It is good that his tail does not move, does not signal warning of any sort. He probably just wants to rest, so soon after the rut. But I am aware, passing him, that I have become more afraid of buffalo than I used to be. I was always cautious. Now what I feel is something more primal. I feel how arbitrary it is for them to let us pass.

Sitting out a rain around the campfire, Wolf says, "I've seen five hundred buffalo along the road. It was different seeing that one yesterday and Dick moving out of the way and then seeing that whole group in the cove. It was different seeing that buffalo today . . ." He raises one hand above the other to show depth. "Seeing the buffalo here was to *experience* the buffalo."

In the backcountry, where the buffalo is not a tourist attraction, but a life, the buffalo is different. We are in his world. We, too, are different.

Although we have cold weather and rain on this trip, it is brilliantly sunny, clear, and warm on the day we ride out, back up Pelican Valley toward the trailhead. Reaching the Pelican Creek crossing, about three miles before the trailhead, in midafternoon, we find a big bull standing on the gravel beach on the far side of the creek. He is standing at exactly the spot we normally come out on our crossing. He stands there, watching.

I think Dick might wait to cross, but he just angles slightly upstream and comes across a little above the buffalo. Once we are all on his side of the creek, the buffalo moves a short way up the easy rise from the creek. Now he stands on the golden grass, watching. Wolf pulls out his camera, excited at getting such a photo. He has never been so close to a buffalo. He is out of film.

176

I can empathize. It's the sort of situation in which you say to the universe, "Wait, I'll be right back, hold everything, keep the moment as it is, I'll go to the store and get film, wait . . ."

"To be so close and have no film . . ." he says.

"It's so your heart will remember," I say.

"I wanted to show my students," he says.

Afterward I am afraid he may have heard my comment as flip, but I have not meant it so. The buffalo so near fills the landscape. There is no frame around him of the sort a camera makes. He is not to be captured; not to become a memory, an object of study. The buffalo, standing on the bank of Pelican Creek, surrounded by the whole of Pelican Valley, is complete. Framed by the earth, he makes a picture so big, it can only be seen with the heart.

SOURCES
AND BIBLIOGRAPHY

FOLLOWING is some miscellaneous information, including addresses, phone, and fax numbers for organizations involved with buffalo and mentioned in this book.

Greater Yellowstone Coalition
13 South Willson Avenue
Bozeman, Montana 59715
(406) 586-1593
Fax (406) 586-0851
Email: gyc@greateryellowstone.org

Lighthawk
The Presidio
Building 1007, P.O. Box 2931
San Francisco, California 94129
(415) 561-6250
Fax (415) 561-6251

Lighthawk Northern Rockies Field Office
31845 Frontage Road
Bozeman, Montana 59715
(406) 586-8572
Fax (406) 586-8572

"Where the Buffalo Roam" is a temporary exhibit housed
in Yellowstone's Canyon Visitor Center. The phone
number for information is the park's main phone number, (307) 344-7381.

The Yellowstone Institute
P.O. Box 117
Yellowstone National Park, Wyoming 82190
(307) 344-2294
Fax (307) 344-2485

The National Bison Range
132 Bison Range Road
Moise, Montana 59824
(406) 644-2211

For general information on Montana's Indian reservations,
contact:

Office of Indian Affairs
Room 202, State Capitol
Helena, Montana 59620
(406) 444-3702

For a brochure listing a calendar of events on the reservations, and specific phone numbers, call:

Travel Montana
Department of Commerce
(406) 444-2654, or, out of state, 1-800-VISIT-MT

InterTribal Bison Cooperative
P.O. Box 8105
Rapid City, South Dakota 57709
(605) 394-9730
Fax (605) 394-7742

For information about the Buffalo Field Campaign, including the video *Buffalo Bull*, produced by Mike Mease, contact:

Buffalo Field Campaign
P.O. Box 957
West Yellowstone, Montana 58758
(406) 646-0070
Email: buffalo@Wildrockies.com

A brief bibliography. There are many more books about buffalo, in print and out of print, that I have not listed.

"How the People Got the Buffalo" from *Old Man Coyote*, Frank B. Linderman, University of Nebraska Press, 1996

The Buffalo Hunters, Mari Sandoz, University of Nebraska Press, 1978

Buffalo Nation, History and Legend of the North American Bison, Valerius Geist, Voyageur Press, 1997

The Bison in Art, A Graphic Chronicle of the American Bison, Larry Barsness, foreword by Barbara Tyler, Northland Press in cooperation with the Amon Carter Museum of Western Art, 1977

The Buffalo, The Story of American Bison and Their Hunters from Prehistoric Times to the Present, Francis Haines, University of Oklahoma Press, 1995

Seeing the White Buffalo, Robert B. Pickering, Denver Museum of Natural History Press, 1997

"Ghosts" from *American Primitive*, Mary Oliver, Little, Brown and Company, 1983

"Coyote and Buffalo" from *Ktunaxa Legends*, compiled and translated by the Kootenai Culture Committee, Confederated Salish and Kootenai Tribes, Salish Kootenai College Press, 1997

Sacred Buffalo, The Lakota Way for a New Beginning, James G. Durham and Virginia Thomas, Sycamore Island Books, 1997

"The Passing of the Buffalo" from *Native American Animal Stories,* told by Joseph Bruchac, Fulcrum Publishing, 1992

Bison, Distant Thunder, Douglas Greunau, preface by Doug Peacock, Takarajima Books, 1995

Yellowstone and the Biology of Time, Mary Meagher and Douglas B. Houston, University of Oklahoma Press, 1998

Bison—Monarch of the Plains, photography by David Fitzgerald, text by Linda Hasselstrom, Graphic Arts Center Publishing Company, 1998

There are three books by Paul Goble, magnificently illustrated stories ostensibly for children, but, in fact, for us all.

Buffalo Woman, Aladdin Paperbacks, 1986

The Great Race of the Birds and Animals, Aladdin Paperbacks, 1991

The Return of the Buffaloes, National Geographic Society, 1996

Acknowledgments

OVER the years I've been following the buffalo, a lot of people have been generous in sharing their information, their ideas, their feelings, and their time with me. Those with whom I do not agree gave as freely as those with whom I do. All of these people are named in the course of this book, but I thank them here, and hope they are not displeased with the use I have made of my experience with them. I am especially grateful to Jeanne-Marie Souvigney, the one person involved with buffalo issues who has never removed herself from involvement, and has always been willing to take time to bring me up to date as well as—with this book—to go over my introduction. I owe thanks, too, to the Greater Yellowstone Coalition for getting me up in the air with Lighthawk and to THE WALL STREET JOURNAL for publishing the original form of *Buffalo Ranch*. I feel deep gratitude to Gena Powell and Richard Clark for their readings of this manuscript in its various stages, and for their honesty; and to Bruce Detrick, whose music is the inspiration for possibility, whose soul is the source of art, and whose reading of my stories makes the stories happen.